Walking Through Illusion

Jesus Speaks of the People who Shared His Journey

An Emotional Biography

First published by O Books, 2010
O Books is an imprint of John Hunt Publishing Ltd., The Bothy, Deershot Lodge, Park Lane, Ropley, Hants, SO24 0BE, UK
office1@o-books.net
www.o-books.net

Distribution in:

UK and Europe
Orca Book Services
orders@orcabookservices.co.uk
Tel: 01202 665432 Fax: 01202 666219
Int. code (44)

USA and Canada
NBN
custserv@nbnbooks.com
Tel: 1 800 462 6420 Fax: 1 800 338 4550

Australia and New Zealand
Brumby Books
sales@brumbybooks.com.au
Tel: 61 3 9761 5535 Fax: 61 3 9761 7095

Far East (offices in Singapore, Thailand, Hong Kong, Taiwan)
Pansing Distribution Pte Ltd
kemal@pansing.com
Tel: 65 6319 9939 Fax: 65 6462 5761

South Africa
Stephan Phillips (pty) Ltd
Email: orders@stephanphillips.com
Tel: 27 21 4489839 Telefax: 27 21 4479879

Design: Stuart Davies

ISBN: 978 1 84694 292 1

A CIP catalogue record for this book is available from the British Library.

Printed by Digital Book Print

O Books operates a distinctive and ethical publishing philosophy in all areas of its business, from its global network of authors to production and worldwide distribution.

Walking Through Illusion

Jesus Speaks of the People who Shared His Journey

An Emotional Biography

Betsy Otter Thompson

BOOKS

Winchester, UK
Washington, USA

CONTENTS

Books by Betsy Otter Thompson

The Mirror Theory
The What Happens if I... Book
You Are What You Think
Lovehuman
Loveparent

To my sisters:
Lynn, Nonnie, and Nancy.
Thank you
For your friendship,
Your inspiration,
And for sharing your journey with me.

GOD THINKS,
GOD LIVES,
GOD BELIEVES,
GOD IS.

Acknowledgements

Shianna
Because you remember the truth when I forget it.
Peace
Because you challenged me to go deeper.
Trace
Because you gave the book more logic.
Liz
Because you brought the book more clarity.
Jesus
Because you simplify what I complicate.

And to all the people who questioned
Because you knew what to ask and when to ask it.

Preface

The heart is a magical organ. It pumps steadily or unsteadily according to how it's treated. If we ask too much of the heart it gives off little signals that warn us of strained love. If the signals are ignored, the heart simply quits; not so different from other motors that aren't well maintained.

Science tells us that hearts depend on the whole through which they function. My instincts tell me that hearts are independent. *Walking through Illusion* was written from my conviction that hearts are free to express from the depth to which they go. Jesus is the energy that comes through my conviction.

What does it mean that hearts are free to express from the depth to which they go? It means that each of us is free to love in the face of reasons not to. If we love, the heart goes deeper to reveal our true identity. If we don't love, more opportunities arrive through which to do so.

I receive inspiration the same way an artist receives a vision or a musician receives a melody. I can't tell you how it happens; I'm not sure myself. However, if I asked a musician how she hears her notes, perhaps she'd say, *I open my heart, I feel what I need to express, and I use my talent to do so.* The same is true for me. I open my heart, receive a feeling, and let that feeling express.

Inspirational writers have different ways of explaining their experiences. Some call it channeling, some call it the joining of conscious energy with the higher self within. Another calls it "a nonphysical energy present in all things that are physical." (Abraham-Hicks Publications–September 16, 2008)

To me, it is the merging of energy. And, in this sense, my energy is merging with the energy of Jesus. When we are together, the best in me is revealed. We all have inspiration to access since we all have hearts that can feel. How it is shared is as individually defined as the individual lives we are living. I believe that a few kind words to another are just as powerfully felt as the creation of a symphony.

My particular gift forces me to acknowledge the physics of action/reaction and the power it wields emotionally in every part of my life. When I first explored these physics, or the pulling of energy back to itself, I saw how it worked in the lives of those around me. Someone I knew behaved a certain way; then another person would behave that way with her. When I asked for an explanation, Jesus said that for every emotional action taken, an emotional mirror returned.

When it came to my life, and how this theory manifested, I denied my culpability, or the possibility that I had given the pain I had received. Had I been that cruel? And even if I had been, hadn't my reasons been justified?

It didn't take long to realize that justification carried no weight in the science of perfect balance. Excuses couldn't change the course of the boomerang. Once it left my aura, it was on its path toward others. In terms of the past and the pain I had created, that was not a happy thought. In terms of the future and the love I hoped to generate, it was empowering.

For the physics of action/reaction to be a viable theory, I had to acknowledge that equal justice prevailed in both directions (whether I liked what I received or I did not). But the more I enacted in positive ways and enjoyed the results I got, the more I tested the power of physics in areas more demanding; more demanding areas were those in which I had caused pain for others. As I faced my actions honestly and acknowledged the mirror returning, I knew that I controlled receivership, at least in terms of emotion. This put me in the powerful position of creating what I preferred.

Awareness of action/reaction deepened my exploration of unresolved emotion. I have lapses now and then, more frequently than I like to admit. They occur when I blame others for the backlash I dislike.

Walking through Illusion is not the usual format for historical reenactments, but like any novel, it is the author's interpretation of possible emotions that might have been experienced. The gift is in the message, whether the history is taken literally or not.

Why were these particular people included in this book? I'm not sure. Some were chosen consciously; some seemed to be chosen for me. As I wrote these stories, I received page by page information that helped me to bring my own life into balance.

Early in the writing Jesus reassured me that these people had lived their lives to the best of their abilities, and wasn't I doing the same. This revelation was important to me because, when I thought of them as somehow different from me, a wall came up between their hearts and mine. When I remembered our oneness, the wall disappeared.

Before the writing began, I believed in a world of rights and wrongs. I saw the picture, or the view I saw with my eyes, as the measure of my existence. When the picture was awful, I thought I was helpless to change it.

Gradually, I learned that all my decisions had brought me growth in one way or another. I learned that taking responsibility for the love, or the lack of love in my life, was the tool through which to create a different experience. My greatest hope is that you will sense your power from reading about these people and create the world of your desires.

Walking through Illusion was not written to challenge historical facts in other worthy books; it was written to challenge me to become accountable. Where once I'd been dealing with guilt, I was finding growth; where once I'd been dealing with hate, I was finding compassion; where once I'd been feeling resentful, I was feeling autonomous.

As Jesus talked about these people and how they hoped to walk through their illusions, as he had walked through his, I asked if they were equally important to him on his journey toward enlightenment. He responded that, yes, they were equally relevant in the moment they entered his life.

The questions in this book arrived through the same process by which the answers came: the union of hearts that promised devotion to one another long before this journey into humanness began.

To introduce the format, I offer the following conversation with my collaborator:

What did walking through illusion mean to you, Jesus?

It meant the process by which I brought a body into illusion to help me remember what was real: emotion, or the part of me that still remained when illusion fell away. Therefore, the challenge was to walk through every illusion with a grateful heart in the knowledge that love was the force that had gotten me here in the first place.

Why did your illusion seem so real if it wasn't?

Because illusion was the game I was playing then. Compare it to an evening at the theater which, incidentally, was my entertainment of choice. Naturally, I became involved in the drama acted out on stage. In the context of that arena, the play was real. However, I knew that, eventually, I would leave that theater and carry on with my everyday reality.

The same could be said of my time here on Earth; it was a play as well. When the play was over, I left that drama and carried on with my new existence, which then became my reality.

How did the concept of illusion versus reality relate to the theater?

The theater was the illusion through which the play was happening; my response to it was real. When the drama was unfolding in the theater, I accepted that illusion for what it was. When the drama unfolded in my life, I sometimes blamed others for the way the play was progressing.

I played a role the same as my friends played a role, and the same as the actors in the theater played their roles–and all of us had chosen the parts we played. Our roles were no more real than the ones we saw in the theater. They were illusionary experiments to expand our hearts so that when we left these dramas, we had the needed emotion for the next performance taking our hearts even deeper.

Were the plays of your friends always valuable?

Their souls must have thought so or they wouldn't have been in them. When the drama was over, they reviewed their scenes, found the growth from living them and moved on to the next play that could further enlighten their souls.

Did everyone achieve the growth they sought?

Some did; some didn't. It all depended on how they viewed the play: whether they took responsibility for their autonomy, or blamed others for the scenes they didn't enjoy.

How could they further their autonomy?

By having faith in their journey; it was designed for inspiration. Without it, they would have been seeking a similar drama anyway. The value they gave their play was the value attracted back. If they didn't like their audience, they had to value differently. Each and every person had a mind that could think independently and, thus, a mind that could recreate until the mirror they loved was present.

Before they arrived to live their roles in this drama, their souls decided when to join the play and when to exit the play. If they shared the love in their hearts as they went from scene to scene, eventually they walked off stage, right into the heart of God forever.

Author's Note

As I began to write this book I wanted to open my heart to different emotional issues, but I only had my own life upon which to draw. I hoped to broaden my perspective and prayed for a way to do so. No sooner had the need been articulated than a group of people entered my life who wanted to read the work. I welcomed their interest and mailed the chapters to them as soon as they were completed. Invariably, each time, one or two would respond with questions of their own regarding how the material related to their particular problems. I responded to their needs in subsequent chapters and, lo and behold, broadened my perspective!

Although these queries seemed to arrive at random, they related appropriately to the chapter being written–and wove into the material as if they had been planned. Many times, a person who had not asked a question would contact me and want to know how I knew of her struggle. I didn't, of course, at least not consciously. Because this happened so frequently, I concluded that the questioner had assumed the role of spokesperson for those in similar straits. I don't know how it worked; I only know that it did. But wherever the questions came from: my imagination, spirit transfer, or literal friends and family, they filled a need in the moment and gave the book a focus that encompassed multiple choices–and that was the answer to my prayer.

If you have questions regarding *Walking through Illusion*, contact me at my web site: betsy@betsythompson.com. You won't be alone in your inquiry. You'll simply be the voice of those who, for one reason or another, were not inclined to speak.

CHAPTER 1

Reform

Where does reform begin?

IF YOU THINK YOU HAVE TO CHANGE OTHERS TO BE HAPPY, NO ONE IS GOING TO CHANGE FOR THE BETTER FROM KNOWING YOU.

What definition did you have for reform, Jesus?

My definition expanded as I did. In my youth, it meant a change in my father's attitude. As an adult, it meant a change in the laws that favored the few. Toward the end of my life, it meant a change within my heart.

Were you alone in your definitions?

No, several friends shared them. Bartholomew in particular had similar definitions since he believed, as I did, that reform was something others needed to do, not something he needed to do.

Who, specifically, did Bartholomew hope would change?

He hoped his father would change, not because his father was cruel and uncaring but because he was narrow-minded in terms of what he deemed appropriate for his oldest son and heir. He and his father both remained inflexible, so friction was ever-present.

From early childhood, Bartholomew had been schooled in the art of diplomacy to facilitate an eventual shift from student to business patriarch. Convinced of his unsuitability to inherit this dubious honor, he vigorously fought his fate, even to the point of faking his stupidity so another son would be called upon to participate.

His father, with tradition on his side, ignored his son's protestations reminding him daily of the heir he was born to be. In fact, the more Bartholomew resisted, the more his father persisted with copious studies of what the job entailed. Bartholomew succumbed to his father's dictates but resented that commitment.

Did Bartholomew resolve this friction with his father?

Not face-to-face. By the time Bartholomew acknowledged that he was the key to any reform in his life, his father had died. Bartholomew now had the business responsibilities, as well as an estate to run. Life to him became a never-ending series of crises that had to be dealt with and a constant flow of trivia that had to be handled. He took his frustration out on co-workers, making them rue the day he arrived.

Relatives, fearful he would abdicate without his father's pressure, offered him a contract they hoped he couldn't refuse. Instead of appreciating his family's faith in him, he did the unthinkable and promoted his brother to take his place.

Thrilled to accept the job, his brother convinced Bartholomew that, now, they both had what they wanted. Apt to agree, Bartholomew involved himself in charities, confident that his purpose would be satisfied through the role of wealthy benefactor. But no amount of giving to the arts and education could heal the hole in his heart. At least in the family business he felt like a necessary part of the process. Now he felt like a money machine.

Had he given out of compassion, he might have enjoyed this role he played. Instead, he gave out of boredom with the intent to buy respect. Not only did he lose the image he wanted, he gained a lot of people trying to buy an image through him.

Discouraged, he wondered if hidden talents had yet to be discovered. Perhaps a role in politics was the answer. The city was in turmoil and platforms were easy to find. Laws were unfairly enforced, leaders unfairly awarded, and the masses unfairly treated.

Politics brought disillusionment, too, for the money at his disposal was the reason he was courted, not the reform he had in mind.

Did Bartholomew's relatives ask him to come back into the business?

Yes. When he declined, he felt like a hypocrite. Here he was living off the earnings, while denouncing the politics that made the earnings possible. His guilty feelings pushed him to rationalize his predicament. *After all,* he muttered, *I want reform; they want the status quo. I want the sharing of riches; they want to keep the riches.*

He wasn't alone in his hope for reform. Several friends were working within the system trying to renegotiate. The government was slow to respond and Bartholomew got impatient. Consequently, he looked outside the system for ways to make a difference. In the process of investigating his options, he came upon a group that called themselves Reformers for Active Peace.

Were you the leader of this group, Jesus?

That depended on who you asked. Some preferred my leadership, some not; most agreed on the nature of the problem, not all agreed on the nature of the solution. The government's ploy for keeping the peace was to punish friends and relatives of those causing the problems. Most of the time, no one claimed leadership; it was the fastest way to get jailed, stoned or crucified.

Was Bartholomew comfortable in his need for reform?

Not always. He was a blue-blood, inside the heart of a rebel. His education and upbringing prepared him to be a leader; his longings took him out of the sphere in which he was trained to perform. Had he stayed in the job and used his influence wisely, he might have enacted positive legislation. But regardless of what he chose to live, he found his growth. If he didn't find it in one arena, his soul created another. But his soul was merciful; it offered the easiest path first.

How could Bartholomew enjoy a job that was filled with meaningless trivia?

When he told himself that meaningless trivia was happening, he couldn't. When he told himself that growth was happening, it was easy. Bartholomew wanted the good life. The good life was one in which the heart found love. Love was found in the moment. When the moment was denigrated, he missed the love it had.

Bartholomew blamed his unhappiness on the job. His attitude was the problem; an attitude that ruled at home as well. His status in the community, and the expectations around it, meant a large and peopled household; in a large and peopled household, servants, relatives, managers, and field hands all had to be dealt with. He knew the welfare of the whole was paramount and touted that principle daily. Still, he had trouble living it.

Instead of offering leadership he offered complaints: *The food isn't cooked properly, the clothes aren't cleaned properly, and the house isn't arranged properly.* Also, according to him, the fields weren't harvested properly. A fetish for neatness made him miserable in the opposite. To Bartholomew, disorderliness of any kind meant a lack of control, and he was very big on control.

If Bartholomew was rich, couldn't he pay to have the services done properly?

He thought so, but an attitude conveying that nothing was ever right made nothing right regardless of the cost.

If the mirror reflected accurately and Bartholomew wanted neatness, did he face other neat-freaks?

He faced other control freaks–and a lot of them were members of this group. They controlled through messes so he didn't see the resemblance. But feeling for feeling the mirror reflected boldly. He thought they were letting their outward appearance influence their inner integrity, (and he had some serious doubts about their cleanliness as well).

It wasn't necessary for Bartholomew to like the messes around him in order to mingle comfortably, but he had to change his mind that something was wrong with a person who did. He could hint for hours that bathing was desirable, but one act of kindness carried more weight than a billion words.

Did Bartholomew see himself as a mentor?

He saw himself as entitled, sure that his privileged background gave him superior habits. Convinced that outward appearance revealed a person's character, he was blind to inner revelations, where true connections occurred. Ironically, he and the messy dressers had the same belief: that others had to change for peace to exist between them–and all believed that dissimilarities were the problem, not similarities.

Wasn't Bartholomew just like everyone else–a person with certain prejudices?

Yes, but prejudice, alone, did not create; the action behind it did.

Did Bartholomew believe his parents were limited thinkers?

In terms of his path, he did. He loved his parents; he just didn't like their values. They had a facade that kept others from looking too deeply into their hearts, and they had good reasons for hoping people wouldn't; especially when they told others how to live, while living as they pleased.

However, their opinions were not the problem; Bartholomew's fear of losing love if he favored a few of his own was. Fear wasn't wrong, just debilitating. What could be strong for them could be weak for him. No universal standard existed, only that which worked for each evolving soul. Bartholomew forgot that inner, not outer transformation was the way to create change.

Headaches began to plague him and he blamed them on the pressure from his family. When he brought his complaints to me, I said that to handle his headaches effectively, he had to handle them in a way that didn't create headaches for others.

Bartholomew listened, but instead of looking within for the cause of his many migraines, he complained outwardly: *People aren't doing what they should be doing; friends aren't making the right choices; and relatives aren't supporting the right causes.* Viewing life through wrongs invited wrongs back, and the body reflected his attitude by manifesting headaches.

Did Bartholomew have to learn a universal truth before he could heal his headaches?

Yes, but for a truth to be universal, it had to be welcomed in every thought God lived. In this regard, the only appealing truth said that energy was free to enjoy whatever truth it had.

See success differently, I told Bartholomew, *and instead of insisting it's something you see with your eyes, see it as something you feel in your heart.* I called this process walking through illusion. When he asked for an explanation, I used an analogy to illustrate my point, reminding Bartholomew that when he visited local fairs, he'd get the llama ride over and over instead of the elephant ride if he only spoke of the elephant ride. He couldn't talk his way onto the elephant; he had to act his way onto the elephant.

He made excuses, saying that a voice inside was keeping him out of sync: *Everyone takes the llama rides so why not you? Everyone complains about them so why not you? Everyone welcomes them so why not you?* I asked him what he was ***doing*** to get the ride he wanted.

Nothing, he said. I replied that life would only improve when he dealt with his own lack of initiative.

Bartholomew hated hearing that he was the source of the problem, but at least it gave him an honest look at what he needed instead.

Did Bartholomew ever find a path that led to comfortable giving?

He finally found comfort in the path he already had by using his inheritance in a wise and thoughtful manner.

Was there another part of Bartholomew's life that often needed healing?

His marriage needed healing, but only because he wanted his wife to be a person he wasn't willing to be: someone who cared about pleasing her mate. Bartholomew's lack of purpose took its toll in this relationship too, as he forced his wife to beg for privileges, even those involved in the smooth running of the household: her responsibility anyway. She resented his interference and withdrew from her duties rather than deal with him. Then she reminded him of the useless person he was, and he got even angrier.

Was it hard for Bartholomew to forgive the people he thought were holding him back?

It was hard for him to believe that no one else could do that; still he resented those he thought were. He finally made a list of all his standing grudges and forgave them for his sake. Then, at least, he was living his own preferred performance.

But even after Bartholomew honored his gift, guilt tried to ruin the fun. *What's the matter with you?* it said. *Don't you know what's expected of you? Don't you know what is right for you? Where is your moral spine? Where is your ethical code? Where is the person you were born to be?*

Did he lose something valuable when the people he loved, loved differently?

He gained something valuable when the people he loved weren't pressured to please him with their choices.

Is it true that Bartholomew died a martyr?

It's true that he wanted to find heaven on Earth. If martyrdom would achieve it, he was willing to live it. In the end, he saw himself as the love of God using illusion to help others find reality.

How could martyrdom bring him heaven on Earth if it meant to lose what he loved?

In that definition, it couldn't, but Bartholomew wasn't losing what he loved, he was finding his truth. Healing was an inward journey; the deeper he went within, the less he needed without. He pursued reality, thereby inspiring others to do the same. Each time he chose reality, he walked through another illusion.

What illusion did Bartholomew conquer?

The one called Matter. Everything seen was illusionary and everything felt was real. When he trusted his feelings over his eyesight, he conquered matter easily.

While traveling, he came upon a culture where the people believed in a different creed. They called their creed The Belief. Because, to them, it was the ***only*** worthy belief, they wanted everyone to take it. When Bartholomew wouldn't, the people got uneasy. Uneasy people wanted to heal. The end of Bartholomew was the healing they sought.

Through a public display of illusionary power resulting in the flaying, beheading and crucifixion of Bartholomew, they thought they had proven their point–that the picture told the whole story, and if Bartholomew looked beaten on the outside, he had been beaten.

Bartholomew honored his truth regardless of how threatening the picture looked and overcame his biggest fear: that of capitulating under pressure; a fate he had suffered before. This time, he lived his integrity and became the integrity he lived.

Would Bartholomew have lived longer had he crumbled?

He might have stayed longer in the illusion to search for his integrity.

What does all this have to do with reform in illusion?

To walk through illusion successfully, Bartholomew had to find the love within it. Once he did, reform had taken place.

ILLUSIONARY REWARD
KEEPS YOU SEEKING MORE AND BETTER
ON A FAIRLY REGULAR BASIS.
BUT ILLUSION WON'T GET YOU
THE MORE AND BETTER THAT SATISFIES.
FOR THAT, YOU HAVE TO APPRECIATE
THE MORE AND BETTER YOU HAVE.

Worksheet Section:

Chapter 1 - Reform

This page is a game for you to play at the end of each chapter. Like any game, there is a beginning, middle and end. Like any game, if you don't play by the rules through which the game is set up, there is little purpose in playing. Therefore, answer each question as honestly as you can and acknowledge the feeling it offers. Then when you reach the end of the game, the feeling you have satisfies.

How many useless goals can you think up?

How often did you laugh while making that list?

List as many meaningful goals as you can imagine.

How often did you cry while making that list?

Anything that makes you laugh or cry is neither useless nor trivial but a vital part of your path. Find the benefits from both.

Questions to ponder:

- *Would I rather have meaningless trivia in my life or no life at all?*
- *Would I rather laugh at my foibles or have them keep me depressed?*
- *Would I rather join the imperfect human race or sit alone in perfection?*

IN ALL THE LITTLE THINGS YOU RELISH ARE ALL THE BIG THINGS THAT MATTER.

Personal Insights

Like Bartholomew, I wanted reform. Like him, I thought I'd have it if the people around me changed. Like Bartholomew, I wanted a different picture to bring it, and like Bartholomew I failed. Also like Bartholomew, I resented those I thought were holding me back. Like him I floundered. As I bounced around on one ride while hoping for another, I battled with the voice of rationalization questioning my need to change. It kept me loveless by saying that I deserved the love I hadn't given; it kept me victimized by saying that others caused my pain; it kept me stagnant by saying that nothing was ever right; it kept me poor by saying that money couldn't be found in the one arena of expertise I seemed to excel; it kept me useless by saying I never had what I needed; it kept me empty by saying a certain person had to show up before I could be happy. Not until I realized that no amount of reform on the outside would solve my problems did I take responsibility for all that I had created. That was my turning point. I knew that if I'd created the mess I was in, I could create something else.

CHAPTER 2

Gifts

What qualifies as a gift?

GIVING TO OTHERS
WITHOUT EMOTIONAL LIFT
LEAVES *YOU* BEREFT OF PLEASURE,
AND *OTHERS* BEREFT OF A GIFT.

Did Bartholomew feel bereft when giving gifts to others?

When he thought his gifts were gone he did; when he knew that his gifts recycled in universal substance and returned with the added power of those who resided there, he was ecstatic.

Did Bartholomew think of you as an important person to know?

In terms of his growth, he did. But I didn't have what looked important, or know those who seemed important–and in Jerusalem, you were nobody if you didn't. What I did have was a deep and abiding trust in action/reaction. I knew that if I acted on the love I hoped to receive, acts of love returned.

Did anyone challenge you to abandon your beliefs?

Everyone I knew at one time or another. Toward the end of my life, when I knew my real identity, no one could force me to sell my honor.

Those who misunderstood my position offered me all manner of worldly goods in exchange for a position they could understand. When I said I already had the world of my desires and it was more wonderful than anything my eyes could behold, they thought I was making fools of them. Here they were offering me the best they had to offer, and here I was saying it wasn't the best

I already had. But the absolute power within was mine; therefore, the absolute power without was meaningless.

Noting my stubbornness and convinced I should capitulate, Bartholomew warned me that my ministry would be better served by making a few concessions. I thought my ministry better served by staying true to myself.

Why do you want my capitulation, I asked him, *when the very reason you seek my presence is because I honor my principles?* Bartholomew insisted that life with me was a lot more important than a few beliefs. I told him that I wouldn't be the friend he wanted if I abandoned those beliefs.

He argued that the government would punish me and that I was sure to suffer. He also argued that he would suffer because of my stubborn ways. I reminded him that suffering was self-inflicted. He conceded that I seemed capable of controlling my pain, but he saw no proof that he was equally capable of controlling his; and he feared what the future would bring. I told him that fear was easily handled by focusing on the love within, not the loss without.

Was Bartholomew respectful of your path?

Not always. He suffered one of his setbacks when he thought a celebrity reputation would further my cause. On and on he went about all the money he would spend and all the benefits he would generate. Caught up in the fantasy of finally making his own life work, he didn't consider mine.

I heard his proposal and told him that all I wanted from him was his happiness to be alive. He was surprised. *Aren't my motives pure: to help you spread your message? Your theories have proven helpful to me. Why wouldn't they benefit others?*

I told him that I didn't care if my theories spread; I was living my theories and that was enough for me. He didn't get it. *To get it,* I said, *you have to switch places with me and ask if you'd want your offering.* Then he got it; not because he didn't want a media campaign behind him, but because he didn't want others telling him how to share his gift.

A well-conceived offering, I said, *is one in which the need is already present; perhaps a coat, a crib, or a carriage is the relevant gift to offer, or maybe even supportive praise for the choices already made.* He tested my words and discovered to his delight, that his needs were automatically handled as he handled the needs of others.

Weren't you capable of creating whatever you wanted, Jesus?

After I knew that life improved by giving gift to others not by getting gifts from others, I was. Happily, when I woke up to the giver within, I was capable of giving myself whatever I wanted.

Was Bartholomew called a rebel for befriending you?

That, and a few other names as well: traitor, loser, hypocrite, and a few even called him ridiculous. Loyalties shifted, and Bartholomew couldn't explain those changes in ways that were understood.

Why did Bartholomew want the government to reform?

Because he thought a better life would result if it did. When he knew how to get a better life, he knew where to go to make it happen. He had to remember that everything given returned. Therefore, a better life was the better he offered others.

Was your youthful behavior used against you at the end of your days, Jesus?

Yes, by my friends as well as my enemies. In fact, some of my so-called enemies were more respectful of me than some of my so-called friends. I was given a hearing, a rare concession for someone of the persecuted minority.

I had something the government wanted: respect from the masses. Respect meant power. Power was desirable. When asked about this power, I said that sovereignty was something found within, and if the officials wanted to control the people, they would have to learn to control themselves. They responded with laughter thinking me hilarious. Imagine saying that they were the ones to change, not the throbbing masses!

Bartholomew was unaware of my hearing with the Bureau. Therefore, when he ran into Samuel, a senator he'd known in his earlier days in politics, he was surprised to hear Samuel say in his best oratorical pomposity that he would personally see to it that anyone who believed the poppycock Jesus was spouting would be rounded up and punished. Terror struck Bartholomew's heart; he knew how the government followed through. In fact, he was so unnerved by this information that he forgot to feign indifference regarding my fate.

Surprised that Bartholomew was concerned about me, and aware of Bartholomew's often eccentric choices, Samuel told Bartholomew that consequences would follow but nothing terrible would happen if I was proven cooperative.

Samuel's definition of cooperative eluded Bartholomew until it was too late. Bartholomew had been finding more and more contentment through introspection; Samuel had been finding less and less through out-inspection.

After this conversation, Samuel became suspicious. *Why is Bartholomew concerned about the fate of this Haggai? Is he somehow involved with these undesirable activists?* Believing it his duty to find out, Samuel arrived on Bartholomew's doorstep a few weeks later. He came in the guise of friendship, as Bartholomew had come to me.

Hoping to bring Bartholomew back into the fold, Samuel pressured him to consider his loyalties, as Bartholomew had pressured me to consider mine. What began as a friendly chat became an interrogation. After an hour of probing questions, Bartholomew knew that Samuel would not be leaving until he got what he had come for. Afraid of being seen as uncooperative and even traitorous, Bartholomew told Samuel what he wanted to hear.

People tried to get through to me at the end of my sermons. Many didn't succeed and sought me out at the end of the day; even in the middle of the night, sneaking through my home trying to find me. When it became disruptive, I suggested to my guests that we make tents out of our beds at night so all would become anonymous.

Bartholomew shared this information but twisted the truth by saying that I was covering my bed at night so I wouldn't be seen disappearing into other realms of existence. He regretted his words immediately and tried to diminish their impact by insisting that he was speaking metaphorically. Samuel didn't care what the words were called. He was looking for proof of eccentricity and he had it.

Was it so far-fetched to suggest that you could do this, Jesus?

Bartholomew never saw me do it, and I never claimed to have done so. It popped out of his unconscious where all was understood. But the conscious mind was so stuck in ego, blasphemy came out rather than praise. When I heard what Bartholomew had said, I praised his imagination and reminded him that whatever he was capable of dreaming up he was capable of living.

Did Bartholomew miss you after you were gone?

At first he did. As time passed and his heart filled with love, he felt my presence. And the more he respected the many ways there were to love, the more of that presence he felt.

Did something wonderful happen to Bartholomew from knowing you?

Something wonderful happened to Bartholomew from knowing himself. His life was full of grace, teaching him what he needed to know. This was the only way his life could be judged–by the ultimate growth it offered.

DISAPPOINTMENT COMES FROM THINKING THAT LIFE SHOULD BE DIFFERENT. ENJOYMENT COMES FROM THINKING THAT LIFE IS WONDERFUL THE WAY IT IS.

Worksheet Section:

Chapter 2 - Gifts

What gift of expression is easy for you to share?

What are you doing to cultivate it?

Is the process working?

What keeps you static?

If the answer involved another person, begin again.

Questions to Ponder:

- *Do my gifts impact matter, or do they impact the heart as well?*
- *Do I worry about my life being useful or do I use my life to love?*
- *Do I curse the disagreers or do I honor what I believe in?*

**CHERISH YOUR AMBITIONS.
THEN IT WON'T MATTER
IN WHICH DIRECTION YOU TAKE THEM,
THE RESULTS WILL BE ENJOYABLE.**

Personal Insights

I couldn't process my thoughts for this particular piece, so Jesus volunteered to clear up any confusion: *Gifts aren't given by a nameless God in heaven, while leaving you alone to struggle here on Earth. God doesn't grace one person with an enormous gift and another with a small one. God doesn't judge the worthiness of any gift that comes through a loving heart. You are the giver, you are the gracer, and you are the judger. You choose the gift; you decide when to express it and how to use it. You can either welcome the gift and expand it, or you can act like it doesn't exist. If you use the gift to hurt another you are the one who suffers. If you use the gift to help another you are the one who benefits. Another's gift may be enjoyable, but true inspiration comes from the way it helps you to sense your own.*

Energy is. Energy is autonomous. Energy is autonomous to go deeper into self, or to take itself back to energy is.

CHAPTER 3

Obstacles

What obstacles stymie growth?

MIRACLES DON'T HAPPEN
BECAUSE YOU BREAK THROUGH REALITY.
REALITY ITSELF IS THE MIRACLE.
BREAK THROUGH ILLUSION, HOWEVER,
AND YOU BREAK THROUGH EVERY THOUGHT
THE KEEPS THE MIRACLE AWAY.

Who dealt with obstacles around you, Jesus?

Peter dealt with obstacles. To break through them, he had to learn that successful fishing was more about waiting than baiting; not waiting for the fish to bite but waiting for the heart to right.

What did that mean exactly?

It meant that for Peter to walk through his illusion in terms of the fish not being available in loving support of him, he had to figure out where in his life his heart was not available in loving support of others.

Was it mandatory for Peter to break through every illusion?

No, but life was more enjoyable when the rules were understood. The rules related to physics. To use those physics effectively was to recognize reality, or the love in Peter's heart as he played the game he was in.

Did Peter see his life as a game?

In the sense that games had rules, wins, losses, and timeframes in which they had to be played, he did. To walk through every obstacle in the human game, Peter had to see the love in every encounter, even the one of sickness, since nothing in the physical world could stop the flow of love. However, until Peter acknowledged that every illness came through his own intentional aura, he wasn't ready to do whatever was needed to heal it.

Are you saying that sickness was an illusionary obstacle Peter had to walk through?

Yes, and we talked about this many times together. Still, he had the mindset that he was not in control of his body in terms of getting sick.

When I shared my theory that health represented a willingness to know the source of renewal, he laughed and said, *I'm having a hard enough time dealing with my theory that colds arrive by chance without dealing with a far-fetched theory like yours.* I then reminded him that "chance" was a theory, too, and whichever theory he took, he got to live.

Did it matter if Peter believed that colds arrived by chance?

Only if he had a cold and wished he didn't.

How could your theory help him more than his theory did?

By putting responsibility where it belonged.

Are you suggesting that Peter got sick when he had sick thoughts?

I'm suggesting that even sickness was the love of God to Peter. His body alone was incapable of deciding what to welcome and what to shun; it welcomed everything. Since the body welcomed everything, healing was impeded when an ailment was unwelcome. On the other hand, when he saw disease as revealing growth, dis-ease turned into ease.

Maybe Peter only said he was sick because he saw how sick he was.

Maybe so, but sickness appeared in illusion. Therefore in reality, something else *was*. Peter had to remind himself that what he was experiencing was the love of God. As the love of God, sickness had a message, e.g., an achy spine could mean a lack of support; a stiff neck could mean a stubborn stalemate; an achy shoulder could mean a painful burden. He had to identify the problem and act on his own behalf to heal it. After he did, illusion moved into reality and the moment transformed.

What could Peter do to find a path with ease?

Ease a path for others. When he thwarted the paths of others, his path became dis-eased. Prolonged dis-ease turned into pain. However, even pain was helpful if it brought him closer to comfort. And whatever brought him comfort was beneficial.

Was it hard for Peter to think of disease as welcome?

Yes, but only because he'd labeled it unwelcome so enthusiastically. He had to call it the love of God with information, and heed its revelation.

As Peter matured and responsibilities grew, he procrastinated. *Tomorrow will be soon enough to heal,* he told himself, *so why worry today*. The only hole in his theory was the persistence of dis-ease. A body that was sick in the moment was a body with an answer for getting well.

When Peter realized that I had conquered illness, he believed that he could, too. His process began when he analyzed as follows: *How is my body trying to help me, not hinder me? Why do I think sickness is love? Who is going to cherish me because I'm sick? Who is going to feel sorry for me? Who is going to regret being mean to me? How is illness forcing me to rest because I won't rest otherwise? If I feel diseased, who have I made feel ill-at-ease?* As he answered these questions and recognized his obstacles, he was able to walk through them.

What did disease represent to Peter?

His belief that he couldn't get what he needed without getting sick to get it. As he recognized those needs, and fulfilled those needs in others, his needs were automatically met. Then he had no reason to get sick.

Did doctors offer healing medicine then?

Yes, and medicine was fine, but true healing came as Peter discovered the reason he got sick in the first place. Then healing was possible without assistance from anyone.

Are you saying that Peter got sick from making someone else feel sick?

Not only did he, it was inevitable; whatever he gave in every category returned for him to experience. He only had to test this theory to prove how well it worked.

What else did fishing teach Peter?

It taught him that it wasn't the size of the fish that made him happy or sad; it was the size of his heart while fishing. When he fished for love, those on shore couldn't wait for the catch. When he fished for reward, these on shore avoided it.

All things being equal, buyers went to the person with more than just food to offer. When the buyers avoided Peter, he prayed for understanding; it came to him in the form of someone living it. *For a profitable day of selling,* I said, *the outing must be filled with the goods people desire; namely, the love wrapped up in the catch.*

Peter believed that his affinity for the sea and his knowledge of the tides would bring him a winning career. It didn't; more sensitivity to the fish and the people around him was needed.

Did Peter's sensitivity increase from being a fisherman?

His sensitivity increased from realizing the difference between what he thought was *catchable* as opposed to what he could catch; the fish were his reflection.

Did Peter's crew appreciate his skills?

Yes, but they didn't appreciate being pushed to the edge of their endurance. Many times they muttered under their breath that Peter would be the death of them. The truth is their safety would have been jeopardized had Peter not been so demanding. Fishing was an arduous profession. Accuracy for details could mean the difference between a safe and productive journey, and ending up at the bottom of the sea. Peter had to be good at what he did and respectful of his ability to pull it off.

Did Peter want to be the best in his field?

Yes, he wanted to be the best. However, when he believed that being the best meant having the biggest catch, the buyers didn't bite. They knew their reward didn't come from the size of the catch, but from the size of the heart offering it. Therefore, they zeroed in on warmer hearts regardless.

As soon as Peter realized that obstacles were emotional, not pictorial, he walked through every obstacle until he found the love.

OBSTACLES ENTER YOUR LIFE
WHEN YOU DEPRIVE OTHERS
OF WHAT YOU THINK YOU DESERVE.

Worksheet Section:

Chapter 3 - Obstacles

What illness often gets the better of you?

What does this illness prevent you from doing?

What does this illness bring to your life that offers some reward?

If you didn't mention emotional growth, look further until you find it.

This is your reality. Focus on the gain and the illness loses importance.

Questions to Ponder:

- *Is my philosophy making me happy or causing me pain and sorrow?*
- *Is my knowledge creating love or is it causing intimidation?*
- *Am I honoring my ideals or caving in at the slightest opposition?*

EVALUATE YOUR JOURNEY
BY HOW WELL YOU HAVE LOVED,
NOT BY HOW WELL OTHERS
HAVE LOVED YOU.

Personal Insights

When Jesus said that Peter had struggled with what he thought was *catchable* as opposed to what he could catch, it reminded me of what I thought was possible as opposed to what I lived. For example, I thought I could have whatever I wanted; the truth is I had whatever I needed. I thought I could marry the person I loved; the truth is I married the person who mirrored my love. I thought I could choose my friends regardless of how I behaved; the truth is I had the friends who behaved as I did. I thought I could capture the essence of inner happiness; the truth is I captured the happiness I was able to feel. I thought I could conquer the world; the truth is I conquered each obstacle day-by-day. I thought I could gain more confidence by achieving something meaningful; the truth is I learned to love myself and found the meaning I sought.

CHAPTER 4

Morality

What is moral and what is not?

YOU ARE
THE LIGHT YOU LET IN,
THE LOVE YOU GIVE,
THE BEAUTY YOU DEFINE,
AND THE REASON YOU LIVE.

Did Peter have a reason for existing?

He had whatever reason he gave himself: *I'm here to be happy; I'm here to be sad; I'm here to serve others; I'm here to serve self.* All were reasons for being.

What was a good reason?

One that made him glad he came.

Was Peter's reason connected to the sea?

Indirectly, yes. He noticed a cycle that not only kept the water healthy, but the creatures within it as well. As he respected this evolution and took only the fish that knew completion, his own completion flourished.

What did it mean for fish to know completion?

It meant for them to experience a sense of fulfillment. Destiny for the fish was to nourish other life-forms. Granted, the fish couldn't ponder, *now I'm ready to nourish,* but they didn't have to; instincts handled that beautifully.

Everything that existed was emotionally charged and capable of fulfillment. Maybe not to the same extent, but not all humans were charged to the same extent either. Peter's only need was to honor his instincts and remember that the young didn't need to be taken for him to earn a living.

His resolve weakened when the number of fish diminished. Then he believed that the number of fish he caught was more important than the number of times he could love while fishing. He also had to contend with a boat full of men who favored a full stomach and a full purse over any law of the sea.

If fish had feelings and all feelings were one, was it moral to kill them?

Peter asked that very question of me. I said I believed that morality was uniquely defined in every moment of history, and each society had its own morality to consider. Peter looked skeptical so I asked him the following question:

If a time existed when human beings could only survive by eating their weak and unhealthy fellow humans, was that moral?

I don't know, he said.

Is it moral to survive on the available food today?

Yes, he said, *but a multitude of food exists upon which to feast.*

True and, at one time, a multitude of sickly humans existed upon which to feast, and, as the only food available.

But you're comparing the eating of humans to the eating of ordinary food.

I am, but morality depends on who is defining that term and how that energy needs to evolve. Cannibalism was once a definition. Granted, if a person in our society made another person his daily diet, his behavior would be considered well below the moral standard. But that doesn't change the fact that, at one time, a person who foraged this way was thought to be the wisest of men. Does that put either of us in the wrong belief?

Not when you put it that way, Peter said.

How else can it be put if God is the wisdom in each of us?

Peter decided that fishing was moral for him in this lifetime, but he wondered how many lifetimes he'd lived in which it was not.

Did Peter focus on his morality?

Yes and morality issues brought his life into focus; especially when he fixated on his income instead of his integrity. Then he lost out on both counts. However, losing a little money was a lot easier than losing a lot of comfort. As he doubted the worthiness of the catch, he doubted the worthiness of the catcher.

Are you saying that Peter struggled with greed?

Yes, and when he was greedy regardless of the consequences to other life forms, others played greedy with him. Friends mirrored this greed by wanting free handouts whether he'd fed his family or not. Workers mirrored this greed by demanding a take of the day whether he'd made any profit or not. Lenders mirrored this greed by insisting on payment whether he owed any money or not. Only after he realized that he couldn't live in one emotion and be mirrored by another did he realize the impact of physics.

Was Peter's friendship with you an easy one?

It got easier when I returned from solitude. Peter launched his boats one day in the face of a gathering storm. Although he knew the outing was risky, the sea was ripe for a haul and he felt up to the challenge. His friends trusted his judgment, and set out to sea as well.

As the storm intensified and Peter lost his way, he had to rely on his instincts to get home safely. Some of the crewmen in other boats didn't fare as well. Peter did what he could to help the injured and thanked the people who braved the storm to help.

As Peter saw me approaching, he expected the same dressing down he usually got from challenging nature's forces. Instead, he was praised for the ample haul he'd made in the face of impossible odds. This was a more accepting Jesus than he was used to experiencing.

Was Peter an aware person at the time of this encounter?

He was a person who met his mirror.

Even though he hadn't been in seclusion?

Are you suggesting that I needed hours at sea to find my inspiration? And if not, why would hours in seclusion be needed by Peter? Meditation was the way within; not the sea or solitude. That's why honoring self was so important; each of us was here to honor our own hearts, not somebody else's.

Peter told me how his instincts had guided him through the storm and I said, *What do you hope to accomplish from trusting this wise and sentient you?*

He said he hoped to share the wisdom he'd found from knowing the sea as a friend instead of an enemy. I told him I was gathering people together to discuss these kinds of issues. And if he wanted to participate, I'd be thrilled to include him.

Weren't you gathering people together to share their belief in God?

I was gathering people together to encourage belief in self. Self was the only place I knew that God could always be found.

Peter was thrilled to be included and, just as he'd been finding the highest form of nourishment in the sea, he began finding the highest form of nourishment in the heart. But wisdom from the former held him in good stead with the latter.

What did Peter sense from attending these meetings?

He sensed a love so pure and deep it overshadowed any fears he had regarding the physical, or the lessening of his strength. When he started equating power with the love of God, he saw no limit on the size he could become.

Did Peter ever stop wanting to be greater than he was?

He never stopped wanting to be happier than he was. The whole of energy yearned for greatness in this respect. As he nourished the energy around him, he nourished himself at the same time. As he strengthened his convictions alongside me, the fish strengthened theirs alongside him.

Did Peter's purpose change throughout the years?

Yes, where once he'd been after a big fat purse and a big macho image, he was after a big kind heart and a big honest love; where once he'd been mining the sea to profit his purse, he mined the soul to profit his heart–and his skills improved as he mined the source.

What did it mean for Peter to see beyond illusion?

It meant for him to see reality, or the love in what he saw. For instance, what was happening to Peter on the inside as he was giving something away?

That depended on why he was giving it.

Exactly; his feelings were his reality. Illusion was the picture of giving something away. Reward didn't come from the act of giving; it came from his enjoyment in the act.

The Earth lived action/reaction but wasn't emotional.

The Earth lived in illusion and was a teacher. It demonstrated on the outside what was happening on the inside to the people living upon it. In the moment of its conception, this planet reflected all that energy knew of itself then. In the moment I lived, it reflected all that energy knew of itself then, too.

Just as our bodies mirrored emotional content on a day-to-day basis, the Earth internalized all that it was offered, pleasant or not, revealing to us the state of our present consensus.

Did Peter struggle to find the love in himself he sensed in you?

Sometimes, but Peter was a man of purpose. When he heard an idea he liked he tested it immediately. In this respect, the sea was an excellent teacher. He couldn't be a good fisherman and a good procrastinator at the same time.

As he learned decisiveness at sea, he used that trait to prove to himself that heaven on Earth existed. But to get that proof, he had to act on his conviction that heaven was possible, not talk about its possibility.

Was it hard for Peter to retire from fishing?

No, it was a beautiful transition full of growth and alignment.

Did he receive your help as his new career paid off?

Peter was a big-hearted friend making his own career pay off. Had he depended on me for the love he sought, he'd still be looking for it.

But Jesus, you seem to be downplaying the role you played in his life.

Because you think of me as the catalyst for making Peter's blissful? I only proved that nothing in illusion could kill the love in my heart. Peter respected that resurrection and got busy creating his own. But his good fortune stemmed from his action, not anything I did.

In the last few weeks of your life, was Peter supportive?

Not always. He sensed my fate. Fearing it would be his, he distanced himself from me, making light of our friendship. Peter hadn't counted on his own sense of integrity, and it brought him to his knees. When he begged for my forgiveness, I told him to forgive himself as soon as possible.

Nevertheless, action/reaction prevailed forgiven or not. Then ego screamed in his ear, *You're the scum of the earth, a loathsome human. Kill yourself, and get out of this nightmare immediately.* He felt tormented but he didn't follow-through. Betrayal returned, however, as the people he loved and believed in denied their friendship with him.

Cowardly behavior was hard to stomach for a man who lived by his honor. He hadn't supported me and he had to live with that fact. But the picture was collapsing all around him and a friend was being crucified for holding certain beliefs.

To be unconcerned, he either had to be so enlightened that fear had lost its power, or so disconnected that feelings were wholly suppressed. He was neither. He was living his life to the best of his abilities, trying to find love and trying to figure things out.

He wasn't prepared to die for a few beliefs; he didn't know why I was. Peter had not yet lived what I had lived: eternal life in the human thought. And since I had proven that death did not exist, my faith was unshakeable.

Why did you attract destruction if you weren't destroying anyone?

I was destroying someone; I was destroying ego, or the absence of love. And I was destroying it quite effectively with every action I took and every breath I spoke. I was able to do this so effectively because of my inner reality, or the overwhelming presence of love.

The fact that ego could counter so forcefully was why I decided a crucifixion had meaning. I wanted to prove that ego could flaunt its ultimate threat: that of death and destruction and, still, love would triumph.

How did you know that love would triumph?

The same way I knew that Monday followed Sunday. I had lived it over and over, and proven to myself that ego was only a voice within, catered to or not.

Did Peter release his old beliefs for the new ones you enjoyed?

Not exactly, he just felt new incentive. Old beliefs told him how to behave and who to love; new beliefs created a person doing so. Old beliefs were philosophical, analytical, and theoretical; new beliefs put them to good use. Old beliefs attracted outer approval; new beliefs created inner approval. He was a man who believed in getting results; therefore, he thrived on the formula getting results for him.

LET YOUR REASONABLE EXPECTATION
BE THE ENJOYMENT OF NOW.
THEN RESURRECTION IS.

Worksheet Section:

Chapter 4 - Morality

What do you hold most dear?

Why do you hold it dear?

Which of your answers related to emotional satisfaction?

If some of your answers didn't, look harder for those that will.

This is how you walk through illusion; by remembering what is valuable, and keeping that focus alive.

Questions to Ponder:

- *Is my history about people, events, and pictures, or how I felt around them?*
- *Is my energy an aging mechanism or an expanding mechanism?*
- *Is my future a picture that has yet to be delivered, or an extension of the moment?*

HOW OFTEN YOU ACCOMPLISH YOUR GOALS DEPENDS ON HOW OFTEN YOU LOVE YOUR ACCOMPISHMENTS.

Personal Insights

The concept of forgiveness has long intrigued me, probably because I thought I had so many people to forgive. Hah! That's before I talked with Jesus. After I talked with Jesus, I got busy forgiving myself. With his caring tutelage, I went from resenting those who had wronged me to loving the growth they offered; I went from wishing people were different to welcoming their uniqueness; I went from hating my lonely hours to loving my independence; I went from hating my current destiny to living the one I preferred; I went from worrying about my failures to appreciating successes; I went from fearing the unknown to embracing each new moment. Nothing changed overnight, but overnight I knew that change was possible. I also knew that I was the one to enact it.

CHAPTER 5

Nourishment

How do we earn support?

**MONEY AS A GIFT
IS A LOVELY FORM OF NOURISHMENT.
IF IT'S AROUND, USE IT WELL.
IF IT ISN'T, MAKE GOOD USE
OF WHAT IS AROUND.**

After you left your body, Jesus, did your friends still feel your love?

If their hearts were open to feel it, they did. My gift to them was the knowledge that they were the same expanding energy I was, and all of us were walking through illusion to help each other sense that beauty within.

Was there one particular person who struggled to feel your gift?

There were quite a few. Often, those who had known me face-to-face found it more difficult to feel my gift than those who hadn't, since they based their guarantee of guidance on their acquaintance with me instead of their acquaintance with themselves.

Those who hadn't known me face-to-face were motivated to search for the reason the resurrection was possible. Paul, of the latter group, didn't witness the resurrection, but he studied the teachings that followed with a dedication matching those who had. As with all teachings, however, they had to be lived to be understood.

Did Paul struggle in this respect?

Yes, especially in terms of give/receive. Frugal to a fault, Paul resisted any theories that threatened his income. But lack on the outside rarely related to money; it related to deficiencies on the inside keeping the outside static. To improve his situation, he had to live the bigness of his heart so the universe could bring him the big heartedness of others.

What enabled him to eventually live in abundance?

His honesty when he didn't. At least when he was honest, he could act on his own behalf to make the moment fuller. When dishonest, he blocked the nature of equal opportunity. For instance, Paul rarely paid his bills in a timely fashion. When he received that mirror, he got angry at his mirror instead of recognizing his mirror.

Did Paul go bankrupt from giving what he didn't have?

No, he went bankrupt from taking what he hadn't given. If Paul borrowed to spread more love around, he made a sound investment; if he borrowed to get out of trouble, trouble expanded. Physics was not a sometimes thing; it worked in every situation, whether Paul was aware of those physics or not.

When did Paul first become savvy about money?

As a youngster when he took to the streets to sell discarded toys. He made such a bundle, his friends were after him to turn a profit for them. His father, discovering his son's entrepreneurial bent, almost fainted. Muggers, crooks, and kidnappers were constantly on the prowl, ready to pounce on the young and naïve at will.

Jacob admired his son's ingenuity but not his judgment. Operating without a license was illegal. In retrospect, Jacob hoped that the system would have been fair to Paul had Paul been arrested, but he thanked his lucky stars that his hopes hadn't been tested.

To give Jacob his due, he saw a gift trying to blossom and, in an effort to help Paul develop it, used his influence to get his son a weekend job in the local tax department. It kept Paul off the streets and busy improving his skills. Upon graduation, he took a full-time position and rose through the ranks quickly.

Earning power grew and so did his investments. He dabbled in real estate, tents, insurance, and even got into the risky business of publishing for a while. But always he was a man looking for answers through funding.

Answers, as in understanding life?

If you call answers, as in understanding receivership. Paul struggled when he made the job more important than the people on the job. Tax collecting or stamp collecting, one career exited for all: discovering the love within.

Did Paul have a mentor?

He had a sponsor. Daniel hoped that hard work, loyalty, and honest dealings would bring Paul success. When hard work, loyalty, and honest dealings didn't reward Paul as much as he thought they should, he did whatever the thought would reward him. Daniel didn't sanction Paul's behavior, but he looked the other way if the money came in.

Young and upwardly mobile, Paul overstepped his bounds on a fairly regular basis. If he got into trouble, he was on his own; his boss wouldn't back him up. You'd think a policy like this would leave the government with a lily-white reputation, wouldn't you–that is, if the people got fooled. But the government couldn't fool the people, then, anymore than it can fool the people now: feelings aren't *hideable*.

Was the government fair?

It asked for a day's work for a day's pay, and in this respect it was honest and fair. Fiscal problems arose from the assumption that taxation would solve the government's every problem. In reality, every problem could only be solved by honoring the power of physics; or by giving the value the government wanted back.

Aren't you speaking of an ideal world instead of the world of Jerusalem?

Ideals enhanced or corrupted even in Jerusalem. Granted, their tax system was not the flawless legislation many hoped it would be, especially in terms of who paid taxes, and who did not. But those who refused to contribute to the services through which they received suffered the indignity of being left out of the activities through which they yearned to participate. The universe was balanced; which meant that any unbalanced whole disintegrated as each part sought new balance.

Action/reaction ran the universe whether it evidenced in a family, a government, a classroom, or a group as small as five people. If Paul took, but didn't give, the universe reciprocated by sending him those who took from him.

To give wisely, Paul had to ask how he hoped to be given to. Then, when the tables turned, which they always did, he received in comfort. When he forgot these physics, he felt unsupported.

He met a man who suggested that he let go of his need to get support, and focus on his need to give support. Paul decided he had a point since there he was, ready and willing to support this man.

Was this man you, Jesus?

No, but this man had known me. While it's true that Paul didn't know me face-to-face, he knew me in the truest sense of knowing. And eventually, he saw what his heart felt.

Was your presence based on faith?

As was everyone's.

Didn't Paul see people to know they existed?

Yes, but had he been blind, how would he have known?

He would have felt them I guess, but wasn't it easier to believe what his eyes could see?

It seemed that way to Paul, but maybe this was the illusion he came here to walk through. I showed myself to Paul many times. Not trusting his feelings, he didn't have the fun of knowing it.

When did Paul first hear about you?

When his friends were discussing my theories. Liking what he heard, he tested a few, particularly the one regarding give/receive. *Okay,* he thought, *I have plenty to offer. What can I give and what will I miss the least?* He gave that gift away and reciprocation followed. The returning gift was useless.

Disheartened, he tested again, giving away an heirloom. Hard as it was to let the heirloom go, a gift of equal beauty returned and Paul declared success. Ultimately, the benefactor regretted his generosity and made his feelings known. He never demanded the gift back, but Paul sensed the remorse in him, which made Paul feel guilty.

In the first scenario, nothing worthy returned; in the second, nothing worthy was felt. Paul insisted that he had done his best, and the theory hadn't produced. A friend, who was also testing the theory, offered a different slant: *Maybe it didn't work according to how you thought it should, but it still worked appropriately. You gave superficially and received superficially. You gave sacrificially and received sacrificially. To receive suitably, you have to give suitably. Emotional growth is the prize.*

Paul tested again, giving to please his heart, and the theory worked beautifully. He only had to remember that action/reaction was emotional and, therefore, his feelings had to be honored regardless of how the picture was evolving.

He had lapses now and then; usually when he felt entitled to one thing or another. He thought of himself as a teacher, and often found himself in front of a group of people giving testimony. Unfortunately, he had a tendency to assume that his audience owed him a living.

After one of these talks, a traveling man, far below Paul's status, came to him bearing a gift of love. Paul took the gift and walked away without so much as a thank you. A few weeks later, Paul's mirror showed up: people assuming entitlement to his time and money. But regardless of how often he pled his case to these debtors, they sensed a taker in Paul and so felt comfortable taking from him. Paul was the one in lack. Therefore, Paul was the one who needed to give in order to have.

Was Paul theatrically inclined?

He never participated in theater, per se, but he speechified when passions ran deep. A preachy attitude, with a touch of intimidation, got him results. Results kept him flush. When he was flush he felt safe.

Did he feel badly when the poor struggled to pay their taxes?

Yes, and although he hated being the cause of lack in others, he liked the feeling of power it gave him. And until he was able to find that feeling another way, he was loath to give up the only way he had.

Did Paul want to feel important?

Yes, and he thought that if others found their importance through him, he would be. After all, if he wasn't this arbiter of others, who was he? A niggling voice inside his head kept him ever off-balance: *Isn't the purpose of your intelligence to guide others? And if so, isn't it reprehensible not to?* This confused Paul until he remembered that to act wisely and with intelligence was to demonstrate someone doing so.

He was well intentioned, wasn't he?

Everyone with him had the same intention: to love. And each person's path was a vision of how to do that.

Was Paul comfortable with his money?

Not always. He reasoned that if I had resurrected and I had been poor, what did that say about those who weren't? He thought he couldn't be holy if he made a lot of money, so he'd lose a lot to satisfy his fear.

Did a different attitude in Paul make it easier for others to part with their funds?

A different attitude in Paul made it easier for him to part with his. He had to change his intention, and instead of taking something valuable away from each encounter, he had to bring something valuable to mark his having been there.

Was that a crossroad?

Yes, it started him in the direction of home.

How did he know that?

Because every place he came to felt like the home he wanted.

**ACTION/REACTION IS A LITTLE LIKE BADMITTEN.
IT ISN'T THE SPEED WITH WHICH YOU SWAT
THAT WINS THE GAME.
IT IS THE FINESSE WITH WHICH
YOU DELIVER THE SHOT.**

Worksheet Section:

Chapter 5 – Nourishment

What support is missing in your life?

What is keeping it away?

How can you turn things around?

What keeps you from trying?

How can you walk through fear and start to manifest?

Questions to Ponder:

- *Do I imitate those who are happy, or only those who speak of happiness?*
- *Do I live a satisfying life, or do I anticipate satisfaction down the road?*
- *Do I look for the best in people or do I look for the worst in people?*

THE SOUL WHO LOOKS FOR SUPPORT RARELY FINDS IT; THE SOUL WHO OFFERS SUPPORT ALWAYS DOES.

Personal Insights

Before I connected with Jesus, I felt unsupported. It wasn't true. I had support; I just didn't like the support I had. Nevertheless it reflected what I had given. Although I felt unloved in the mirror of my behavior, it offered a means of comparison. Then when life turned around, I knew the difference between the uneasiness of the past and the comfort of the present. Before I lived that turnaround, I almost became a bag lady. Two caring people intervened and gave me loving support. It was awful. It was wonderful. It woke me up. From that moment forth, one question remained: How can I give the support I so hope to receive? As I used the power of action/reaction to get the mirror I wanted, the power of action/reaction grew. Not that life is perfect. I still get disappointed now and then; mostly because I focus on what is missing instead of what I have.

CHAPTER 6

Beliefs

How important are beliefs?

**EVERY SCENARIO
IN WHICH YOU'VE FORGOTTEN TO LOVE
IS WAITING FOR A MIRACLE.**

How did Paul define a miracle?

Eventually he saw it as a thought transformation.

A thought transformation in what sense?

In the sense that his thoughts were moving out of resistance and into love. Pictures often supported miracles but they couldn't make them happen. Miracles occurred when the loving side of his nature was honored, even when another side seemed to be more appropriate.

Did he have many hurdles to overcome?

Yes, but hurdles were overcome by seeing reality, or the love in every heart.

Could miracles happen when the people around Paul were awful?

The awful people around him were the miracles waiting to happen. Paul had many catalysts in this respect; Nero being one of them. But Paul didn't see Nero as a catalyst. He saw him as a murderer; a man who believed that anyone weak enough to fall prey to the powerful deserved to suffer the consequences.

Wasn't it hard to think of miracles with a messed up person like this around?

Yes, but it was fertile ground. Messed up pictures lived in illusion; reality was the love he found regardless.

As a young man, Paul found Nero engaging. As Nero broadened his base in cruel and sadistic ways, Paul condemned his tactics. Paul wasn't alone in his critique; plenty of tax-paying discontents agreed. When Nero heard about these critics and knew they were gaining converts, he found a way to punish them. Hearing about their fate, Paul got uneasy. But when nothing happened to him, he declared that nothing would. After all, he was a prominent citizen and couldn't just disappear. More importantly, Nero had once been a colleague. Surely Nero would honor that acquaintance. Paul miscalculated. Why would Nero honor a friendship Paul did not?

What did Paul hope to accomplish by damning Nero's tactics?

A separation from Nero, but condemnation was the very activity Nero was engaged in; therefore it did the opposite. Picture for picture, Paul's cruelty looked tame compared to Nero's. Emotion for emotion it felt the same. He wasn't even angry to Nero's face, only behind his back. But illusion couldn't be more than it was: illusion. And illusion couldn't separate that which was real, or emotion. Therefore, Nero received Paul's anger, even when Nero lived one place and Paul lived another. He also received all the anger Paul stirred up in others because of him.

Would Paul have believed Nero's sincerity had Nero spoken compassionately?

Probably not, but if Paul had given Nero the benefit of the doubt, others would have given him more of theirs.

Did Nero ever do things differently?

Not in Paul's lifetime but even if he had, it wouldn't have altered Paul's experience. For that, Paul had to do things differently. If he wanted compassion instead of cruelty, he had to stop giving Nero all the hate Nero deserved, and start giving Nero all the love Paul deserved: exactly the hurdle that had to be overcome.

Hard as it was for Paul to admit that he mirrored Nero from critiquing Nero behind his back, miracles could only come from acknowledging this reflection.

Why was Nero cruel?

For the same reason most people were cruel; he felt threatened. If Nero wanted to live his miracles, he had to realize that life wasn't cruel or sadistic if his soul wasn't burdened likewise.

Paul must have felt justified for his feelings regarding Nero.

He did, and Nero felt justified for his feelings regarding Paul. But justification didn't stop the force of physics.

Convinced that his condemnation was defensible, Paul reasoned as follows: *Isn't God involved in my beliefs? And isn't God judging the good and the bad, the kind and the cruel, and the wrong and the right? And if God is, shouldn't I be on the side God takes?* Confident of his position, he embraced the role of advisor, not only with Nero, but with the people he called his flock.

When some of these people disagreed with Paul, he warned them of dire consequences if they didn't fall back in line. When they continued to rebel, Paul called them ignorant disbelievers, too dense to get the point. But to doubt their wisdom was to doubt his wisdom. Then he missed the only point there was: that getting it had to do the depth of his heart, not the depth of his I.Q.

Was Paul disadvantaged from not knowing you in person?

If bodies lived in illusion, why would that be a drawback? Closeness to me in my lifetime was found the same way it was found in Paul's lifetime: through the sharing of similar emotion.

Paul was living in judgment not release; therefore the body reflected his attitude as dis-ease became disease. Hoping to heal his frequent bouts of malaise and nasty rashes, he summoned the healer, Echias, a man who offered a blunt and stubborn mirror if ever there was one. Paul interacted with Echias as he interacted with others, as a man whose purpose it was to convert. Echias responded to Paul by saying, *Why would I want to take your beliefs if they're making you so sick?*

Paul was dumbfounded; what did his beliefs have to do with anything? Ignoring Echias, he complained about a cousin he didn't like. Echias, ever responsive, said, *What do you want to do, kiss this man goodbye forever?* Paul said no, he just wanted him to shape up. Echias said, *Show him how to and maybe he will.*

Paul wanted to be right more than he wanted to be well, so even though Echias warned him that constant bickering was ruining his health, Paul continued to bicker. Echias understood something Paul did not: that a quality life had more to do with emotion than it had to do with beliefs.

Did Paul anticipate a beautiful reward from converting men like Echias?

Yes, and he anticipated a reward commensurate with the number of converts he had. But while he waited for future bliss, he lived uncomfortably on Earth.

Wasn't it only natural for Paul to want to share his beliefs?

It was only natural for him to want to live them. More to the point, if he was happy in his beliefs, why did it matter who else had them? Paul believed that justice pertained to later, or when he met his maker. Convinced that the more converts he had, the closer he'd be to God, he rationalized any temporary grief for a final reward in heaven.

A *suffer to get* philosophy was quite in vogue in those days. Many thought it led to more enlightenment. *Wasn't Jesus a martyr,* they argued, *and didn't he sense a better fate awaiting him? And if something better awaited him and he'd martyred himself to get there, wouldn't it profit us to martyr ourselves, too*? Caught up in that logic, Paul told himself that *now* was not important and everything should be done for *later*. *Later* brought him the shock of his life; there was no *later*.

What do you mean? Paul dropped his body and then it was later.

He dropped his body and it was still now. The heart didn't live in time, it lived in emotion; and emotion was eternal. Therefore, when he joined eternity, everyone with him before he left was with him after he left, including me.

How could he realize that?

How could he not? The instant Paul knew there was only one place to be, he knew everyone had to be there. When he asked for his reward, I told him to look inside his heart and find it. Paul saw a lot of strangled emotion around should's, could's, if's, but's, and maybes. Viewing the human experience as a stepping-stone to something greater, he missed the greatness in matter.

When he asked me why I'd found such love from being a martyr, I asked him why he thought I was a martyr. *Because you let yourself be killed,* he replied.

If I let myself be killed, I said, *I must have known that tomorrow was the same as today, and whatever I felt in the moment was mine the next moment, too.*

Paul mentioned the suffering I must have felt. I told him that suffering was a feeling I got when not enjoying the moment. In this respect, he had suffered more than I had. I had loved those moments, while he was always waiting for love to come.

Did you put your nerves in a coma or something?

I put them in the light of love where perfect health resided.

Wasn't there more to it than that, Jesus?

Paul wondered the same thing, so I offered him the following analogy: *You think nothing of water evaporating in the presence of high heat. Well, heat to me was the love of God, and the warmth of that presence was every bit as powerful when it came to transformation.*

Did Paul call your resurrection a miracle?

He knew I'd found love where he hadn't found it, so it fit his description. But to me, the resurrection was a vehicle; a way of authenticating my beliefs. Granted, my method of doing so was unfamiliar to Paul, but that doesn't mean it was any less satisfying to me.

At one point in history, plenty of people were living the vision I enjoyed at the end of my life: that of total nourishment, with the body sustaining itself through the power of love. In fact, they did it for eons. Because I understood the properties of *birth, exit, rebirth,* and knew it as the natural state of being, my resurrection was possible.

What other state of being did Paul struggle to understand?

The state of being a Christian; he wanted to be a faithful Christian but he couldn't live up to those standards. Christians were taught to be selfless. He wasn't. Christians were asked to think of others before themselves. He didn't. Christians were told to act with charity at all times. He couldn't. Christians were asked to tithe. He wouldn't. Christians were told to dig deep for compassion, work hard for honesty, and toil long for redemption. His success in all three was minimal. When he heard that Christians were supposed to think of themselves as lesser than saints, he wouldn't concede to being lesser than anyone. Christians were asked to be generous in their praise, missionary in their behavior, and meek in their hostility. He was a disappointment in all these as well.

As far as he could tell, the only thing he did better than Christians was die, and even that fell short; for it turned out there was no such thing.

LOOK DEEPLY INTO THE HEART OF TODAY TO SEE THE FUTURE CLEARLY.

Worksheet Section

Chapter 6 - Beliefs

Write down a few of your childhood beliefs.

Which ones still work for you?

Which ones don't?

Why?

Didn't each of your beliefs work for you in some meaningful way while you had them?

Questions to Ponder:

- *Do my beliefs make me happy, or am I happy when I love my beliefs?*
- *Does happiness come from pushing my love on others, or from pushing myself to love?*
- *Have I evolved as much as I want to, or do I hope to evolve even more?*

**SOMETIMES THE BEST THERAPY
IS SIMPLY BELIEVING THAT
EACH DAY IS EXACTLY AS IT SHOULD BE.**

Personal Insights

Why are people convinced that their beliefs are so important? Do they assume that those beliefs will get them into heaven? And if those beliefs aren't making them happy now, why do they think they will sometime later? My beliefs have gone through several radical changes–from a complete and absolute faith in the Church, to agnosticism, to a belief that love is the only power worthy of recognition. And frankly, none of the above made a particle of difference in terms of how my life was going. Life went according to what I accorded others. And you know what? I strongly suspect that, when I leave here, future happiness will have the same criterion.

CHAPTER 7

Opinions

Can we control our opinions?

REMEMBER YOUR FIRST OPINION?
REMEMBER WHAT HAPPENED TO IT?
REMEMBER WHY IT CHANGED?
EVERY BELIEF IS MEANINGFUL
UNTIL ANOTHER ONE COMES ALONG
TO LOVE YOU MORE.

Did you respect other people's opinions, Jesus?

When I respected my own, I did.

Did any of your friends have trouble with respect?

Yes. Matthew had trouble with respect. He worked for a government that rarely hired Jews. Since both the Jews and the government were intolerant of each other, he invited pain from two different directions: fellow-Jews who shunned him and fellow-workers who cursed him; the former from doubting his loyalty, the latter from hating his heritage.

Did Matthew ask for advice regarding his job?

Yes, but advice was only worthy if it highlighted the benefits.

Was Matthew the only government employee in his family?

No, his father Alphaeus worked for the government, too. His brother, Seth, had tried to, but hadn't lasted a week. Unable to restrain himself when the insults came his way, Seth retaliated with insults of his own. An apology was demanded, but Seth quit rather than give one. Matthew and his father had worked for years to establish the family's loyalty, and one foolish act on Seth's part had set them back a decade. Matthew warned Seth that should the family suffer as a result of his poor judgment, he would be held accountable. Convinced that he was justified, Seth would not relent. In his opinion, he'd only defended the good name of his family. Matthew, older and wiser about the ways of the world (although not so wise about how to handle Seth) responded to Seth's naiveté by listing every misstep his brother had ever taken, whether it happened a day ago or a year ago. Reeling from the unfairness of that attack, Seth took to the streets, stirring up trouble where Matthew was trying to keep the peace.

Angry that Seth was making a difficult job even harder, Matthew was beside himself; not only because of Seth's behavior, but also because his boss was not amused: *How can I trust your ability to control the Jews if you can't even control your own brother?*

Worried about his family and if they were at risk, Matthew came to me in a panic. *How can I maintain order with Seth determined to mock it, and why is he so intent on being disruptive?*

I told him that if Seth continued getting attention for his disruptive behavior, Matthew should expect to see a lot more of it. *Highlight his strengths instead of his weaknesses,* I said, *and let the focus shift.*

Matthew was incredulous. On top of everything else, he was supposed to coddle Seth? But willing to try anything, he thought, *Okay, there has to be something to praise in Seth, even if I have to stretch the truth to find it.* When Seth received that stretch, he called Matthew a hypocrite.

Was Matthew's approach wrong?

Not wrong, just delusional. Why would Seth react favorably to condescending remarks? Matthew was so distracted by Seth's antics he failed to notice the fault-finding person he had become.

Are you saying that Seth's betrayal was not the problem?

I'm saying that Matthew had yet to name the problem. Phony praise was not a cure-all; it was a destroy-all. Matthew had to admit to his own caustic delivery instead of lashing out at Seth's. But regardless of who got blamed for the circumstances, they needed healing, and too much loyalty in either direction could mean disaster for all.

Taking the initiative, Matthew decided that, of course, Seth had attributes and therefore he would find them. Happily, as soon as Matthew declared that assets existed, they were easy to see. Seth performed many kindnesses for the people around him: small favors to assist his mother, helpful tips to boost his sister's confidence, and time-consuming errands for an overworked staff. As Matthew praised genuine acts of kindness, Seth felt his approval. To Matthew's everlasting astonishment, Seth needed less and less attention as Matthew found more and more praise. Soon, there was nothing left to heal; Seth didn't object to hearing how nice he was. In fact, he loved it.

What other worries did Matthew have?

He worried that he'd never be free of blame regarding the government's decisions. When fellow Jews attacked him because of their anger with the government, Matthew used the same tactics to cope with them that they were using to cope with him, and started blaming anyone he could think of.

His parents were handy candidates, so he accused them of forcing the job upon him. Not willing to be the scapegoat, his parents gave him back as good as he gave. Matthew hated their anger, so he was loath to dissent.

He had to sift through his emotions and find the truth. Had he taken the job to please his parents or had he taken the job to please himself? He couldn't answer that question with any degree of honestly for quite a few years.

When I told Matthew I was leaving home to live my dream of

travel, Matthew's ambiguity grew. In me, he saw a person taking responsibility for his future, and making decisions independent of family. In himself, he saw a person answering to his family in a job he couldn't enjoy.

Who am I living my life for, anyway, Matthew asked, *my parents or myself? And if these people aren't living their lives to please me, why am I living mine to please them? Why can I disengage so easily from some of their dictates and not from others?*

Trying to be supportive, I reminded Matthew of several reasons the job was beneficial: the healthy income generated, and the chance to play the role of strong protector. Still he resented the consequences and refused to become accountable.

I'm not responsible for the person I am or the job I have. My parents did this and my parents did that. My parents said this and my parents said that. How can I be other than who they have forced me to be?

Even though Matthew was caught up in excuses, I knew his opportunity was the same as mine: to decide the direction in which to take his future.

Did Matthew think you were preachy when you told him about your plans?

No, but many times over the years he had thought I was preachy.

When did Matthew first hear you preach?

When I was about six. Naturally, my themes matured as I did. But, if I was preachy around Matthew, he didn't hesitate to confront me. Once, when he was struggling with the abuse of fellow Jews, I looked him square in the eye and patronizingly told him that inner healing had to be found before outer healing could manifest.

He shook his head from side to side, rolling his eyes incredulously. To him, inner healing seemed incidental compared to the horror he saw with his eyes. Was he supposed to be nice for the sake of niceness because the high road was the *good* road? The scales weren't balanced and everyone knew it. Niceness wouldn't change that.

Defiant, and tired of hearing me preach, he looked me square in the eye and said, *I'll believe in your theory of healing when I see your healing manifest!*

Did Matthew blame the government for the persecutions of Jews?

He blamed the Jews for persecuting him. He was well aware of the moral dilemma his job created for Jews, but he hoped to prevent a greater evil by living a lesser evil. Later, he chronicled his version of history as a means of atonement, hoping to justify all that he'd chosen in the name of love.

Was Matthew a lifelong friend or yours?

Yes, but the friendship wasn't steady; it lapsed when one of us had growth that was incompatible with the other.

What brought the two of you back together?

I was struggling with my detractors and Matthew arrived to offer support.

Did Matthew consider you a goody-goody while you were growing up?

On the contrary; he considered me a mischief-maker. Joseph often sensed that imp in me lurking beneath the surface threatening to express. Then he would pile on the work to keep me busy. I resented his demands and often complained to Matthew that Joseph was more intent on controlling me than respecting me. Years later I was still complaining when Matthew retorted with a line he'd heard me using: *Well, if you weren't so intent on controlling others, maybe his behavior wouldn't bother you so much!*

Was Matthew surprised when you involved yourself in controversial issues?

Heavens no. For as long as he had known me, I'd been challenging the status-quo, and often rather flamboyantly. Even within my craft I was extremely avant-garde, not only trying new tools but creating new tools. Joseph often objected to the time it took me to make them, but he knew a good gadget when he saw one.

Did Matthew's parents feel threatened by his friendship with you?

Yes and many people did, whether they knew me well, hardly at all, in the past, or in the present. When fear got a hold of people, they did just about anything to get rid of it, even betray a friend.

How did Matthew react to parental fears?

Once again, he found himself in the middle of clashing loyalties: not only with his family, but also with a public that found me appealing, and a government that did not.

Did Matthew see you when you returned from traveling?

No, but he saw me when I returned from solitude. Mildly curious, he came to hear me speak. Then he was madly curious. I still spoke of the beauty of God, the power of love, and the balance of give/receive. But now I was living my talk. As I demonstrated the integrity I hoped to see in others, I became a magnet to those seeking theirs.

Although the government thought that popularity interpreted into power, Matthew knew that, to me, power represented the depth of a loving heart. But for Matthew to keep that focus while trying to keep the peace put a whole new twist on the challenge.

Jews were attacking him, kicking and beating him daily, venting their rage at him because they couldn't vent at non-Jews and still hope to survive. Matthew went to his superiors and asked for their support, but they didn't concern themselves with any private wars he waged. He found it hard enough working for people who hated him, without the Jews attacking him for the politics of the government.

Did his friendship with you challenge Matthew to find more integrity?

Befriending himself was the key to that enlightenment.

But you were in his life.

And so were many others. Those who benefited from knowing me were those who tried what I tried. Those who didn't refused to look within as the source of what they needed. I had the same challenge Matthew had: to recognize my mirrors and do something about the ones I hated. If I didn't, I had lots of heavenly concepts rolling around in my head and lots of unpleasant mirrors to deal with, too.

Was Matthew upset when you were crucified?

Yes; to him, it was the end of his friend and mentor. To me, it was the rebirth of love.

Was there any one incident that helped Matthew to notice the power of give/receive?

Yes, one occurred in his childhood. He saw himself as a nice kid, honest most of the time with a father in a well-placed government position and a mother active in charities. The family enjoyed privileges; one of them being the fancy school Matthew attended.

Often, Alphaeus and Matthew would come to my father's shop with items needing repair. If I wasn't doing a chore, Matthew and I would pal around together.

That particular morning, Matthew and his mother were meeting with the tailor to go over clothes for school. Alphaeus appeared and ordered Matthew to come with him instead. As tactfully as possible, his wife explained that the tailor had arrived and was waiting to serve their needs. Ignoring her, Alphaeus ushered Matthew out the door. Embarrassed but respectful, she carried on with as much dignity as possible.

When Matthew and his father arrived at our shop that day, I was playing with other friends. Accustomed to having me to himself, Matthew begged me to go off to the park with him. Reluctantly, I agreed. No sooner had we arrived than a few of Matthew's friends from school showed up. Convinced he would be ridiculed for being with the likes of me, Matthew said he was playing with riff-raff since no one else was around. As soon as the words were spoken, he felt my mortification, his friends' embarrassment, and everyone's disgust with him. Needless to say, I left.

Matthew tried to bond with the new arrivals but they soon found excuses for getting rid of him. Instead of returning to Joseph's, he walked home alone resentful. When I got home, I told Alphaeus in all my self-righteous indignation that Matthew had found other friends to play with, and was not returning to the shop. Embarrassed by his son's behavior, Alphaeus took me home with him to confront his son directly.

Then it was Matthew's turn to be mortified. Not only had he gone through the initial torture of treating me badly, but here he was being tortured again. Furious to be so confronted, he lost his temper and blamed everyone else for this awful predicament. But the universe brought him exactly what he had given–with a little extra thrown in for good measure.

Matthew could call himself honorable and praiseworthy until he was blue in the face but the universe showed him who he was regardless.

I lived my mirror that day, too, and for the same reason he had. After all, I'd pulled a similar stunt in the morning with some of my friends.

Alphaeus blamed his anger on Matthew; Matthew blamed his anger on Alphaeus. In truth, both were angry with themselves.

But instead of looking within to explain their rage, they raged at each other. When Alphaeus calmed down, he told his son that life was not about praising himself but about honoring his praiseworthy friends.

Alphaeus sounds very wise.

He'd be delighted to hear you say that, but he would remind you that he lived his mirror that day as well; experiencing the same embarrassment in front of his friends that he'd caused his wife in front of hers. But even in the midst of turmoil, he was learning to recognize the physics of action/reaction and the power it wielded emotionally in every part of his life. Since he was here to learn what the universe had to offer, it showed him its gift at every opportunity.

Wasn't Matthew being punished for a lack of awareness?

It may seem that way, but how could awareness blossom if action wasn't reciprocated? When love was felt, he wanted that feeling to grow. When pain was felt, he didn't. Cause and effect was his safety valve. If he ignored it, the future felt unpredictable.

If Matthew believed tomorrow had love, did that make it so?

Tomorrow had love whether he believed it would or not–just as the moment had love whether he believed it did or not.

When Matthew left this plane, he was focused on the future and all that he hoped it would be. But time disappeared when he left illusion, so there he was stuck in the moment whether he liked it or not. However, once he knew that *now* was all there was, he got busy making it beautiful as quickly as possible.

Will Bible historians agree with this story, Jesus?

To be a Bible historian is to be well acquainted with all that is in the Bible. To be God is to be well acquainted with all that is in the heart. The Bible shares the love of God; millions of books do the same. The absolute from which they all birth has no favorites. Believe in the worthiness of all, and all that exists will feel worthy to you.

Did Matthew have any talents?

He considered himself something of a poet. Perhaps this rhyme can cherish you.

FOR EVERY HILL YOU CLIMB IN LIFE
THERE'S CHANCES TO SUCCEED
FOR EVERY HILL YOU CLIMB WITH GOD
THE BOUNTY WON IS THEE.

TAKE HEED OF WHERE YOU KEEP YOUR THOUGHTS
AND FIND THE ONES THAT PLEASE YOU
CAUSE EVERY TIME YOU MISS YOUR MARK
YOU'RE GIVING OUT A MIS-CUE.

Worksheet Section

Chapter 7 - Opinions

Who are you blaming for all the wrongs in your life?

If these people change, will your problems be over?

If others choose to love, whose life improves: yours or theirs?

How can you make positive changes without any help from others?

Who will be grateful if you do?

Questions to Ponder:

- *Am I looking for revenge or am I looking for love?*
- *Am I looking for someone to blame or someone to praise?*
- *Am I hoping to be right or am I hoping to be healed?*

SOLUTIONS ARE SELF-INSPIRED
AND ALWAYS WILL BE.
PROBLEMS ONLY EXIST
TO PROMOTE INNER GROWTH.

Personal Insights

I appreciate honesty, especially if I have asked for it. However, several times when I did ask for it, I reeled from that truth when I heard it. I was devastated on one level, relieved on another. In fact, the relief was so enormous it overshadowed the pain. I didn't know why at the time. Later, I realized that the God in that person had spoken. I recognized the speaker and relaxed. We all get challenged to be honest. Roadblocks, in the guise of fear, sometimes get in the way, e.g., you'll only get hurt, you'll hurt another, you'll be in a jam, you'll make things worse, you'll only be judged, you'll lose what you want, you'll lose what you have, you'll make others mad, and so forth. The truth is that if we are honest when we are asked to be honest, we offer the greatest gift there is: the chance to let the God in us express.

CHAPTER 8

Approval

Is approval necessary?

IF YOU WANT TO BECOME A TEACHER, YOU MUST LIVE THE LESSONS YOU PREACH.

Did you go through a time of wanting approval, Jesus?

Yes, but seeking approval attracted people seeking mine. To get approval, I had to give approval; especially to myself.

Who else overcame this obstacle?

Mark overcame this obstacle, as he conquered the odds by living the unlikely and doing what he'd previously only talked about.

How did you meet Mark?

Through a mutual love of traveling; he wasn't a preacher in the same sense that I was, but he eventually lived his talk, which made him every bit the example I was.

What did it mean to live the lessons he preached?

It meant to be a master instead of telling other masters how to be; exactly the hurdle he had to overcome. For years he preached the art of horsemanship to anyone who would listen. Unbeknownst to his listeners, he hadn't accomplished the basic step of getting atop a mule.

Ashamed of his phobia and fearing its discovery, he camouflaged his frailty by conversing like an expert. Then he was a preacher without any mastery. To become a master, he had to stop talking as if he were an expert and get on a horse to become one. After he conquered this challenge, he thought he'd lived a miracle since judgment about it had tyrannized him for years.

The mastering technique was the same regardless of the mastery and involved the following principle: *if you think up an idea it exists. If you live an idea, it's yours.*

What if Mark wasn't brave enough for the living part?

Then every experience came to make him braver. Resistance only grew from a fear of what he'd find. What else could keep him from mastering that technique and going wherever it led him?

Eventually, he emerged victorious, at least in terms of getting atop a mule. He didn't stay mounted long, but the fall was a lot less painful than the fear attached to trying, so back on the mule he got and tried again... and again... and again. Granted, the mule was not a horse but it was close enough to make him feel empowered.

How did Mark view his early efforts at mastery?

He viewed them as his test rides, telling him where, when, and how to make adjustments.

Did he understand why he felt compelled to learn to ride?

He assumed it was because of his need to trek from one farm to another in his effort to earn a living.

Was itinerant farming respected?

Not on a scale of careers to be admired. Most people chose to live close to family and friends; those who knew and loved them. Familiarity had a certain predictability factor that eased the harshness of living. One couldn't predict what might be encountered ten miles from home, nor was the average farmer eager to learn what did. Just as in other societies, the strange and unusual was criticized, and for that reason alone.

Mark saw drifting as a weakness, or an inability to adjust to life as it was. A voice inside tormented him: *This isn't quite the place you need to be; these aren't quite the people you need to know; and these aren't quite the influences you need to experience.* Then he was always looking for the one place that would be the place he sought.

Did Mark want the respect of others?

Yes, but he tried to get it by pointing the finger at other drifters, hoping if they were seen as less together, he'd be seen as more together. All he ever got was the finger-pointing of others. Rather than deal with all these pointers, he moved on to new farms in search of different people. But there he was in front of himself no matter how many moves he made.

Are you saying that he never got accepted?

I'm saying that whether he did or not was irrelevant. He couldn't feel accepted if he hadn't given acceptance, regardless of how many people offered it. He had to get into the vehicle he hoped to enjoy: approval, and start living its properties.

What did Mark discover from searching for answers in so many different places?

More reasons to analyze where they came from; a place within himself.

What did Mark hope to achieve?

Distinction, but without any permanent residence, education or influence he thought he couldn't achieve it. Fearful of being ridiculed for having silly ambitions, he ridiculed those succeeding where he had not; labeling them distracted, exactly what he hated hearing about himself.

Did anyone tease Mark because of his need to travel?

Yes, but any obsession they had revealed their needs, not his.

Was it healthy to let a goal consume him?

Why not? Would he have found the songs he loved, the books he cherished, and the paintings he revered if the makers of them hadn't made them important? Mark had to learn that goals couldn't be realized through speaking a lot of words, and no one wanted to hear him talk about that which wasn't even working for him. Enthusiasm was contagious on a temporary basis, but without any action behind it, it wasn't taken seriously, by him or anyone else.

What did Mark think of you when he first heard you speak?

He thought he'd met a man who shared his every conviction. Years later, he met a man called Peter, recently from Jerusalem, who was speaking of a healer by the name of Jesus. Mark didn't ask Peter if I was the same Jesus he had previously met, but an answer came anyway, as talk of miracles greeted him at every farm he worked.

Many itinerants were leaving the fields to follow-up and investigate. Unwilling to make that commitment (and envious of those who were), Mark talked incessantly about the idiots who were going. Then it was even more difficult to follow his heart because he didn't want to look like just another idiot doing the same.

A voice inside thwarted his ambition: *Your presence in Jerusalem is meaningless; you're too low on the ladder of humanity to matter to anyone, even if you go.* When he realized that going was for his sake, not somebody else's, love won the argument.

Could any worldly circumstances have changed his need to go?

No, but everything he'd lived up until then was helping him understand why.

What reasons did he have for staying away?

Jerusalem was urban and he was country; the inhabitants were sophisticated and he was naïve; the city was militaristic and he was peaceful. There wasn't a thing about the city that appealed to him except for the presence of those with similar concerns.

Eventually, he couldn't resist the pull to go any longer. When he got there, the city was all he dreaded it would be, but much to his surprise it didn't matter. He got so caught up in what Jerusalem had to offer, he forgot to notice its lack.

When Mark found me and introduced himself, I was chatting with several friends. Curious about this man, we asked him why he had left the fields to pursue a life in the city. He told us his story, and mentioned several itinerants who had left the fields before him. But instead of praising their paths, he spoke of them disrespectfully. The next day, he heard these men speaking of him disrespectfully. He came to me and complained. I suggested that Mark thank these men for sensitizing him to the complainer within.

If Mark preferred the rural life, why was his destiny to end up in the city?

He considered it a worthy challenge. Would he be strong enough to put the illusion behind him and follow his heart? The fact that he did, and focused on the self-love that had gotten him there, was quite a feat after all the fear he'd attached to going, and all the ridicule he'd attached to those who had. For years, Jerusalem had been the last place he could see himself being, but because he made that courageous leap of faith, it became the best place for living his growth.

Did a miracle come to Mark because he moved to Jerusalem?

The miracle came as he realized that every move he'd made had gotten him closer to self-approval. He eventually accepted the obvious: Who better to assist Jesus on his travels than someone who had done a lot of his own? With his mule, he could ride ahead and prepare the way. This role as guardian journeyman was all that he hoped it would be. He came to realize that nothing he'd ever lived had been wasted or meaningless, which turned out to be the catalyst he needed for trusting the future.

Did Mark question the purpose of your traveling?

Yes, and I told him it allowed me to serve the people who liked my purpose.

Was he a groupie or a hanger on?

He hung onto my words a lot. But I was living autonomously by the time Mark moved to Jerusalem; therefore, those who didn't found little support around me.

Did Mark learn to accept his mirrors graciously?

He struggled like anyone when he didn't accept his mirrors as being accurate. It was easy to acknowledge the beautiful mirrors; difficult to acknowledge the opposite. He learned to be honest by focusing on the feeling he had instead of the person who had caused it. Then he was able to trace that feeling back to the moment he'd given it. When he honored that first flash of insight, he saw himself in the answer. When he didn't, ego diffused the truth by keeping him focused on others.

When did a place become important to Mark?

When he noticed the growth it offered; when he didn't, he wasted his time. Time wasted caused a disconnection. A disconnected mind focused on outer images instead of inner images, where true connections occurred.

What if a place had nothing worthy to offer?

Every place was the same place until Mark realized that progress was emotional.

Did he miss traveling after he settled in Jerusalem?

Outer traveling paled as inner traveling prevailed.

Did he live alone in Jerusalem?

Until several relatives came to live with him. Mark told them about the people he'd met and what they had achieved, and his family urged him to hire a scribe to write those stories down. He decided instead to hire a tutor. But even then, more literate souls were needed to make the narratives readable.

Did Mark wonder how a poor migrant's definition of ultimates would be received?

Yes, but he watched a poor carpenter live his and found help through example.

Did he live the right path for the wisdom he sought?

The right path was a path that offered love.

How many paths offered the love that people really needed?

Every path that existed; some found help through a guru, rabbi, priest or minister, some through a philosophy, some through nature, some through friends, some through artistic endeavors, some through a trade, some through everyday living, and so on.

Mark traveled from sight to sight to sight until he realized that places couldn't bring him growth. For that he had to travel from insight to insight to insight. As he learned to love his choices, he faced others in the same appreciation. Together, they bolstered each other's faith in their walk toward oneness.

When Mark passed on, did other souls still judge him?

Not by refusing to communicate. Emotions weren't *hideable* in a world defined by feelings. When he passed on, he realized that out-of-body souls didn't always agree on the nature of thoughtfulness any more than in-body souls did. Those differences got resolved as each soul did what it thought was helpful.

What did Mark see in you that he hoped to achieve in himself?

A peaceful heart. When he asked me how I'd found it, I told him that peace had come when I recognized myself as the source of all my answers.

Did you then became Mark's teacher?

Mark then realized that if he loved himself as I did, he'd find his own.

YOU CAN'T FIND ANSWERS IN ILLUSION
NO MATTER HOW MUCH OF IT YOU HAVE,
HOW BEAUTIFUL IT LOOKS,
OR HOW LONG IT STAYS AROUND.
BUT IF YOU NOURISH YOUR FEELINGS
WHILE IN ILLUSION,
THOSE FEELINGS LEAD YOU TO ANSWERS.

Worksheet Section:

Chapter 8 – Approval

In what way are the people around you less than you?

In what way are the people around you greater than you?

In what way are the people around you equal to you?

Which of those answers would you like to share with others?

How would you change your answers if you knew they were received, spoken or not?

Questions to Ponder:

- *Who am I? A body that turns to dust or a soul that turns to trust?*
- *Where is comfort? In the approval I get or in the approval I give?*
- *Where is fulfillment? In the feedback I think I'm due or in the joy I generate within?*

OPINIONS COME AND GO,
BUT THE HOLDER OF THE THEM
IS A NEVER-ENDING STREAM OF CONSCIOUSNESS.

Personal insights

Like most children, I longed for approval. My mother, thinking praise unhealthy, did her best to keep me well. Her attitude was partly generational, partly genetic, and partly a desire to keep me humble. But whatever reasons she had for her behavior I still longed for approval. Years passed before I realized that her needs mirrored mine. She longed for approval, too, and was just as confused about how to get it as I was. In her struggle to find it, she saw my behavior as damaging to her progress. In my struggle to find it, I saw her values as damaging to mine. Happily, by the time I made my most outrageous choices, I knew that progress couldn't come from her approval; only from self-approval.

CHAPTER 9

Fairness

Why is life so unfair?

IN-MATTER OR OUT-OF-MATTER,
THE FAIRNESS YOU WANT,
IS THE FAIRNESS YOU NEED TO GIVE.

How could you think the same fairness was needed in-matter as out-of-matter, Jesus?

How could I not if matter was illusionary and therefore temporary, and fairness was emotional and therefore permanent. That which was permanent was real, and only the real could impact my life.

Who struggled with fairness around you?

John struggled with fairness. And he did because he refused to see the difference between speaking of friendship and being a friend. I suggested that he love the people around him, not because they deserved to be loved but because he deserved to be loved.

Did fairness relate to money for John?

Sometimes; especially when he associated money with security. Money was always scarce for John. In an effort to heal that scarcity he moonlighted as a grave digger. When I heard him cursing his fate, I proposed that he find the benefits from grave digging instead of the drawbacks, so the benefits could expand. Wanting desperately to do so, he came up with the following pluses: Yes, the work was tedious but at least he was working; plenty of people were not. Yes, the income was meager but at least he was helping his family; many workers were not. Yes, his poverty went bone-deep, but poor on the outside didn't necessarily mean poor on the inside. Yes, his status in the community was lowly, but it offered insight that many high-status jobs did not; namely, that outward beauty shone briefly, while inner beauty lasted forever in the hearts of those who felt it.

Did John eventually find the fairness he thought was so important?

Yes, but only after he realized that *importance* was an idea he had about himself, not an idea others had about him.

Did he charge a fee for his grave digging efforts?

Yes, but whether he did or not didn't seem to matter; those who wanted to pay paid, those who didn't, didn't. Eventually, he took the position that people could pay whatever they thought the job was worth. It wasn't very businesslike, but it sure took the pressure off of waiting to be paid.

Why shouldn't John expect to be paid?

He did expect to be paid. But the universe didn't react to his expectations; it reacted to his enactments. John tried to duck out of paying others for their services, therefore others tried to duck out of paying him for his. When he gave unconditionally, support returned and he fared much better. *More* didn't necessarily come from grave digging, nevertheless it came.

Did you help John to understand the fairness he needed to give?

I helped John to notice his mirrors so he could help himself. He grumbled about the unfairness all around him and how it stuck in his craw, so I suggested that he play fair with others to get to know that feeling. He instantly thought of several people who deserved more fairness from him, but instead of using that information to improve his behavior, he used it to analyze theirs. As a result he had lots of critical opinions and minimal change within.

Was John a philosopher?

In the sense that he wanted others to think of him as wise, he was. When he wasn't seen as wise, he spoke of how wise he was anyway. When ordinary words fell short, he tried extra-ordinary words. Small in stature, he wanted his talk to do what his looks could not. When that didn't work he tried intimidation: *Come to John if you want to feel safe in a world full of darkness and evil. Come to John if you want to avoid the plague. Come to John if you want to be saved from the wrath and punishment of God.*

Seen as unworthy in society's eyes, he promised hell to those who ridiculed him and heaven to those who didn't. I promised him neither punishment from above nor hell from below; I promised him the mirror of the moment.

Did John ever love himself enough to stop being a gravedigger?

He loved himself enough to stop making it wrong that he was.

Before he came into his body, did he anticipate good results?

Before he came into his body, he knew that any results would be up to him: *Will I have the courage to follow my heart? Will I enjoy my choices once I do? Will I respect the choices of others? Will I remember the nature of support, and will I be able to live it once I have?*

Did John want the reassurance that he could survive this journey?

Yes, but until he knew that survival depended on what he could feel instead of what he could see, insecurity mounted.

Wasn't survival a physical thing, Jesus?

No, physicality was illusionary; reality was emotional. Emotion couldn't die of old age or be killed by a sword.

But swords had a way of stopping one's path, didn't they?

Temporarily. In fact, one ended John's. But whatever he knew how to do, he knew how to do. Therefore, if he'd gotten himself here once, he could again. Not as the person he was, but at the end of a sword, a new idea was timely anyway. The recipient was once the giver even in swordplay. John didn't literally stab a person to attract a stabbing back but he used his position as a well-known healer to make another feel sick. She received that heart-felt wound and wanted revenge. When Herod promised her a favor, John's beheading was the favor she exacted.

Did John antagonize Herod, too?

He set himself up as the person to whom Herod should answer, and that annoyed Herod. John's problem stemmed from the fact that he critiqued people without regard to the consequences. Then he was critiqued without regard to the consequences.

Plenty of people agreed with John's assessment of Herod, but agreement didn't stop the force of physics. Action/reaction related to emotion. John made the mistake of thinking that God was on his side and, therefore, he could do whatever he pleased and God would handle the consequences. He got what he gave regardless.

Are you saying that God was not on his side?

I'm saying that God didn't take sides. John saw God as an outer power, protecting him from evil. John was the God who had to protect himself. He believed in a vengeful God, not a compassionate God. When he felt compassion in me, he was forced to reassess the nature of God's true heart.

Why did your compassion force him to reassess?

Because I was getting everything I wanted with compassion as my tool. John was blaming his neediness on his poverty. His history was that of a man scrounging for a living and bickering for the upper hand in a cutthroat world of have and have-nots. I felt his pain and offered him a room in my home as a temporary solution. Then ego had a field day:

Where can I cut a few corners to gain an advantage? How can I use the services in this household so I won't have to pay for them elsewhere? Who can I get to do my duties so I can spend time with Jesus? How can I benefit from the presence of people here; never mind if they benefit from mine. But every time John thought he had what he needed to satisfy his longings, someone would come along and satisfy his by taking it.

In an effort to ingratiate himself with the people in the household, he convinced himself that a housekeeper had outlived his usefulness and he was the one to take his place. Guilt followed and the psychic battle began. The loving side of John didn't want to hurt this man; the needy side didn't care. *Forget about his problems,* it said, *you have enough of your own.*

Thus began his campaign to undermine the opponent; criticize here, nit-pick there, ostensibly to show how right he was for the job. At first John was seen as helpful. As persistence grew on his part, resistance grew in others. Once, when he grabbed the broom and criticized the sweeping, someone came over, gave the broom back and said, *No one cares how well this job gets done; only that he have a chance to contribute.*

Another time, he took the duster to show the housekeeper that he, John, was better at reaching the corners. Someone came over, gave the duster back and said, *It isn't the cobwebs in this house that need your attention, but the cobwebs in your head that keep you from seeing the love in this beautiful soul.*

John felt crushed, not because of the words he heard, but because he was crushing another. Nothing improved until John realized that he'd never feel useful while making another feel useless.

Conceding defeat, he accompanied me on my travels. The first thing he noticed was the obvious angst in others and how they wanted to feel useful, too. In his effort to grow, he gave a few kind words to those he'd previously ignored. Nothing elaborate; he didn't want to sit in failure again.

Positive action became an upward spiraling euphoria getting better and better just as negative action had been a downward spiraling fall getting worse and worse.

He heard me compare the cleansing of our souls to the cleansing of our bodies and converted that into tangible reality through an outward and visible ritual representing an inward and spiritual goal: the purification of spirit. He used what was readily available, easily handled, and appropriately symbolic: the loving use of water. John called it baptism.

After that, he became the official baptism administrator. Each time he performed this simple ritual, he remembered how a gift was born: not through the aping of another's gift, but through the joyful expression of one's own. By honoring his imagination, he found a way to expand his friendships, use his intelligence, and support the whole at the same time. He also had sessions where people could talk about their problems, ask questions, and share their hopes and dreams for the future.

John still wasn't rich in the worldly sense, but he redefined abundance as the size of his heart, not the size of his income.

Did John charge a fee for his services?

Yes but he didn't reject anyone who couldn't pay.

Did he feel guilty for charging?

Guilt was a byproduct of refusing to support other people's services, not a result of charging for his own. Whether a person paid or not, John received his due.

Was anyone else allowed to baptize?

No one took baptism seriously enough to claim proprietorship. Anyone could do it. John hoped it would spread, for if it was fun for a few, it would be fun for many.

What kept other baptizers from leaving John bereft of a job?

The hundreds of people who wanted to be baptized; as the fun caught on, other communities wanted to participate, too.

Are you talking about John the Baptist?

Some people called him that but other Johns baptized. John ritualized and organized the concept. He never claimed to have started it, just to have found inspiration through it.

Did John care if someone else was credited with starting it?

He only cared that people were loved through their own form of cleansing, for this was the joy he got to share with them.

YOU DON'T FEEL SUPPORTED
BY WHAT YOU GET FROM OTHERS.
YOU FEEL SUPPORTED
BY WHAT YOU GIVE TO OTHERS.

Worksheet Section:

Chapter 9 – Fairness

How do you bring more love to the lives of those around you?

How do you feel while making that contribution?

Is it a feeling you want to expand?

What keeps you from trying?

Have you forgotten that valuable contributions are emotional in nature?

Questions to Ponder:

- *Am I hoping to belong to the consensus, or, to my inner senses?*
- *Am I happier when people agree with me or happier when agreement is moot?*
- *Am I asking for love with my talk, or giving love with my talk?*

PEOPLE FEEL COMFORTABLE IN YOUR PRESENCE WHEN YOU FEEL COMFORTABLE IN YOUR PRESENCE.

Personal Insights

I believe that I choose to be close to God, not that God chooses to be close to me. I believe that God is available to everyone, not just to those who follow a certain path. I believe that God loves everyone equally, not just those who seem to be good, holy, and righteous. I believe that God blesses all who work to achieve a goal, not just those who seek out "holy endeavors". I believe that we come here to share the love within, not to conquer the without. I believe that heaven resides in individual truth, not this truth or that truth. I believe that God is in every faith, religion, and philosophy if the participant has a heart full of love.

CHAPTER 10

Curiosity

What are we searching for?

**IF YOU SEARCH FOR GOD OUTSIDE YOURSELF
THE SEARCH WILL NEVER END.
TO KNOW GOD'S LOVE IN HUMANNESS
THE SEARCH BEGINS WITHIN.**

Did it take John a long time to search within for happiness?

It took him as long as it took to search everywhere else. In the interim, he robbed the dead to fill the void. *How can it matter?* he reasoned. *The mourning families are reconciled to being without their valuables and nobody knows what I'm doing. At least I'm putting food on the table, and securing a future for me and the rest of my family.*

But stealing for profit was a self-defeating hypothesis; the mourners sensed his actions and reacted. To appease his guilty conscience, he convinced himself that his family's needs superimposed any penance. However the pain became so excessive, he fell down on his knees in prayer: *Dear God, give me a sign. Show me the way. What can I do that will profit me more than stealing?*

His prayer was answered the very next day when several gold pieces were left behind in a casket. Determined to honor his prayer, he didn't dig them up. Later that week, he received a tip that far exceeded anything that particular grave could have rendered.

I rejoiced in John's good fortune but he didn't respond. Sensing his confusion, I reassured him that God saw him as a pure and loving soul regardless of his choices. When he still didn't respond, I mentioned that perhaps this was his opportunity to look at life differently.

What do you mean, he demanded. *Pretend that life is wonderful when it isn't?*

Life will become whatever you tell yourself it is, I responded.

Why should I believe you?

You have just proven why. You believed a better way existed, and a better way materialized. What other proof do you need?

After that, John tried to see himself as a man gaining insight instead of a man losing status. He made up stories about the bodies he was burying: how they had lived, who they had loved, what they had loved, where they had lived, and what they had learned.

As these fantasies took root, he sensed a connection he hadn't felt before and was able to wish these souls a bon voyage. Whether or not they heard him didn't seem to matter; he'd found a way to honor his hours productively.

As his interest grew in the people he was burying, his interest grew in the families who had loved them. As they received his interest they couldn't help but respond. Gradually, he stopped feeling like a third wheel at these eulogies and began to feel like a necessary part of the ceremony. It finally dawned on him that happiness had little to do with the job; it had to do with the way he was handling the job.

Did children and babies participate in baptism?

If the parents wanted to include them, they did. But baptism wasn't for babies; it was a pledge to honor self, which babies already did.

Who was allowed to baptize?

Anyone who wished to. As soon as a person said, *Who qualifies to baptize and who does not,* the love it represented was less than it could be. As the benefits of this ritual made an impact, John realized that love was self-inspired and always would be. And once he knew the responsible party in terms of his enlightenment, the real party began.

Did he consider baptism a prayer to help children prosper and live more wisely?

As long as the meaning of prosper wasn't restricted.

Did John hope that people would choose this sacrament?

He hoped that they would love what they were choosing.

Was baptism about forgiveness?

It had any meaning a person wanted to give it. If John chose forgiveness, it was a new beginning for him. The forgiven had to do their own forgiving to beget new births.

Didn't people's lives improve when you forgave them, Jesus?

Why would people need my forgiveness to gain a better life?

Well, if they had wronged you, causing you horrible pain.

If pain was in my heart, I was the one keeping it alive.

What if you forgave a person and released her to begin again?

Was it really release if I said to her, *I forgive you for all the horrible things you did to me?* Wouldn't that really be saying, *Regardless of your awful behavior, I'm holy enough to overlook it and move on?* Now you tell me, was that release or judgment?

Healing didn't come from announcing: *I'm the holy forgiver and you're the unholy blackguard.* It came from remembering that everyone deserved what I deserved: a chance to begin again.

Did you ever use the idea of water when you were teaching?

Yes, in fact I shared a vision, a vision of walking beside the sea; a sea so beautiful that its very essence excited my curiosity and delighted my sense of adventure. In this vision, a hat was on my head that held all the information I'd ever wanted to know, and because the hat was inclusive, I was filled with wondrous feelings.

As I wandered along the shore, I got curious about the water and waded in up to my ankles. Wading was so exhilarating I went a little deeper. My head was still above water and the hat still firmly in place. Curious about the depth below, I dipped my head beneath the surface, leaving my hat behind me, sure that when I wanted the hat back, it would be waiting for me exactly where I had left it. Depth was quite enchanting and full of discoveries, too, but I got a little confused about where I was and what I was doing since the knowledge hat wasn't with me.

My friends on shore got curious and, soon, hundreds of them were in the water, exploring this new depth. Some couldn't function without their hats and went back to get them immediately. Some ignored their hats as the underwater experience became the measure of their existence. (But even in this perception, happiness was possible if that choice was being appreciated.) Some remembered their hats and were moving toward them steadily. Some couldn't find them and were frantically trying to, and some were swimming around in the water with their hats on, helping others find theirs.

In this analogy, could you fully explore the water with your hat on?

Yes; the water experience was the same regardless of how much of me was in it.

Was it ever good to forfeit the hunt?

John thought so since he didn't appreciate his hat until he'd lived without it for a while. To keep the hat in every new adventure, he had to stay in touch with the knowledge it held. Entering deeper had risks as well as benefits. The water was alluring, but it was also very temporary. Too much faith in the temporary and the real was hard to remember. Then it took a lot of swimming and searching to find the hat again.

For a truth more permanent, John had to consider the speed with which water evaporated in the presence of any heat.

Why couldn't John take his hat with him under water?

Because the hat represented knowledge; water could only support things.

Was water a metaphor for life?

No, water was a metaphor for matter. Sometimes matter was; sometimes not. Matter had many sizes, shapes, and densities but held no lasting truth; it changed as the atoms split to enjoy more diversity.

Did John eventually find his hat?

His energy did. Then he sat in total recall. In total recall, oneness was. Part of that *oneness* was autonomy. In autonomy, he could choose any game he wished to. But the same thing happened in all of them. He played until his heart was content and on he moved to another.

Before John came here, did he hope that his journey into the water would bring him a lot of love?

Yes, but to find that love, he had to claim the hat already known as his. He entered this game for enlightenment the same as everyone else. Survival was not the issue. He existed whether the water game was or not.

Was it possible that John would never find his hat?

No, his reunion was inevitable. When this particular search became exhaustive, he temporarily abandoned it. But the hat was still there, waiting for him to claim it. As soon as he was ready to re-ignite the search, he jumped back into the water and reestablished the hunt.

What was the nature of John's hat?

Knowledge of God's powerful energy. He only left it behind from a need to explore the unknown. The love he found in each new adventure became a part of his hat. Believe it or not, a time existed when all were playing in the water with their hats firmly in place. In fact, they did it for eons. For John to understand his essence, he had to look beyond the finite to explain his light-filled potential.

Did you find your hat, Jesus?

Yes; I reached an awareness where nothing in the water interested me any more.

Did you know the content of other people's hats?

I only had access to mine. I could sense what others hadn't sensed yet, but the truth was there for both of us. I only had information about other people's hats to the extent that I knew all hats were one.

If a psychic saw into John's future, wasn't she seeing into John's hat?

If a psychic was wearing her own hat, she didn't need to see into John's. Hats held total information. In total information, God was revealing the relevant. When John visited psychics, he had to remember that love spoke with compassion. If a message arrived without it, he had to check out the informant. The opposite of love was ego, and ego was trying to be heard, too. He only had to remember that like-feeling auras attracted one another in every aspect of life: friend, foe, or psychic.

Did John have any moments when the love in his hat was felt?

He had many moments when the love in his hat was felt. John struggled because he believed that unconditional love would make him even more vulnerable than he already was. But had he loved unconditionally, he would have found his mirror.

Was John using people by putting conditions on his love?

He didn't like it when others bargained with him over theirs, so yes, I'd say he was.

Was John's love conditional for those who were out-of-matter?

Yes, but matter was illusionary; real connections occurred emotionally.

What would have happened had John loved unconditionally?

He would have been living in the water with his hat on.

**FAITH CAN'T BE BOUGHT, BARTERED, OR BEGOTTEN.
IT IS THE KNOWLEDGE OF WHO YOU ARE,
WHY YOU ARE HERE,
AND HOW TO ENJOY THAT SEARCH.**

Worksheet Section:

Chapter 10 - Curiosity

How do you honor the lesser positions around you?

How do you honor the greater positions around you?

How do you honor your position?

If all the lesser positions suddenly became the greater positions, would you alter your answers?

How can you honor both in appropriate ways?

Questions to Ponder:

- *Am I kind because it's expected of me or because it makes me happy?*
- *Am I happy because of the knowledge I hold or because of the joy it brings me?*
- *Am I blessed because of the money I have or because of the way I use it?*

REALITY CAN'T BE FELT UNTIL YOU KNOW THAT EVERYTHING SEEN IS ILLUSION.

Personal Insights

I've done a lot of swimming in search of my hat, sometimes against the current. Once or twice, I almost succumbed to the undertow. Nevertheless, on I went, hopeful that eventually the water would calm and settle. Sometimes it did, sometimes not. When it didn't, I tried to go with the flow instead of fighting upstream. When I succeeded, my attitude improved and I could see the benefits of the current I was in. Water has a built-in struggle factor. If I do nothing I sink. I have to at least doggie paddle to stay afloat. I can lie on my back and hope to feel some buoyancy but that doesn't work if the water starts to churn. Then I have to go with the flow anyway.

CHAPTER 11

Truth

Whose truth is the right truth?

NO ONE ELSE'S BELIEFS HAVE VALIDITY IN YOUR LIFE UNLESS YOU LIVE THEM, LOVE THEM, AND THEREFORE UNDERSTAND THEM.

Did you struggle with your truth, Jesus?

Sometimes, especially when it seemed that everyone else had a different one. When I lived my deepest truth, no one could sway me from it.

Who challenged you to honor your truth?

Thomas challenged me.

Was he a good friend?

That depends on how you define friendship. Was he constant in his presence? Yes. Was he always supportive in his constancy? No. In fact, he often betrayed our friendship, not by maligning me behind my back, but by holding onto the Jesus of the past instead of the present. He missed the Jesus of his childhood; the Jesus he understood. And he wanted that Jesus back. Angry that he couldn't make it happen, he cursed what he thought the reason: a truth in me he didn't understand.

Thomas had a choice: he could belittle what he mistrusted, or he could use his doubting nature to expand a truth he loved. Regardless of which he did, he lived the role of doubter to such perfection that, eventually, it defined his very essence.

Were Thomas' parents helpful in combating his doubt?

No, they were the combatants he chose for encouraging doubt. And they lived their role to perfection, too, doubting everything about him: his interests, humor, looks, memory, avocation, instincts, intelligence, just about every aspect of existence. Thinking praise a sin, they did their best to remain holy.

How did Thomas respond to their doubting natures?

He was reactionary, seeing them as the bane of his existence. When he heard me speaking of willful choices, and not distinguishing between those that were made before we birthed and those that were made after we birthed, he was skeptical. It didn't make sense to him that he would have chosen vindictive parents on purpose.

Didn't their mentoring lead you to seek new mentors, I asked him. *And didn't the new ones lead you to seek new growth? Isn't it only logical that had you wanted more positive influences, you would have chosen them? You chose the opposite. Now you need to understand why.*

My parents victimized me, Thomas responded quickly, *and I wouldn't have chosen victimization on purpose.* I suggested that growth had been his choice since victimization was a non-viable concept in a perfectly balanced universe. Thomas argued that growth was impossible if all he did was suffer. I suggested that he hadn't opted for suffering; he'd opted for enlightenment, but if it took suffering to reach it, so be it.

Did Thomas have strong opinions about you?

Yes and he had a right to his opinions, but opinions were only suppositions; he had no knowledge of the inner journey I was here to live.

Was he a doubter as a child?

Yes, the pattern started early when he couldn't find a better way to protect himself from his parents. He talked about their cruelty and, when I heard him complaining, I asked him the one question he couldn't refute or debate. *If you chose your parents in complete understanding of the challenge they offered, and the only one to blame for their presence is you, is blame a viable concept? If it isn't, flip-flop your definition of liability and, instead of insisting it's something your parents have toward you, think of it as something you have toward yourself. Instead of pinpointing all the ways these people have ruined your life, highlight all the ways they have pushed you to find a new one.*

From this very compelling thought, he found some very compelling answers.

Was it hard for Thomas to release his old beliefs?

It was as hard or as easy as he let it be; a simplistic answer, yes, but answers with merit usually were. First, he had to trust that change was possible; then he had to follow through and make it happen. His beliefs didn't change overnight, but overnight he knew his beliefs could change.

Immobilized by a tape in his head playing his parent's predictions, he attracted people playing similar tapes. Anger kept them hostage and used them rather badly; so it wasn't any pathway to heaven, that's for sure.

Even after a different truth emerged, the challenge continued. Those who had known Thomas in his old beliefs hated him taking new ones–so they tried to drag him back to the old ones; exactly the challenge he had given me.

Determined to manage doubt more constructively Thomas announced to a group of people that he was sick and tired of viewing the world through cynicism, and would view it through trust instead. No one believed him, of course; the room was full of doubters. But as soon he acted on his intentions, the universe sent him those acting on theirs.

Would his path have been easier had different people been with him?

Different people were not the problem; dealing with self was. First Thomas had to handle his own negative aura. Then he made it easier for others to handle theirs.

Did his friends respect his doubting nature?

Reactions were individual. Mark, for one, enjoyed Thomas' presence because lively debates followed his friend everywhere he went. Matthew enjoyed Thomas' presence because people focused on Thomas' arbitrary nature instead of his.

As a frequent target of Thomas' convoluted arguments, Peter was less sanguine; he dreaded trying to figure out what in the world Thomas was asking. But regardless of other people's reactions Thomas was in his element in any kind of debate. The irony was that no matter how many times he diverted the conversation away from cause and effect, I brought him back to physics eventually.

Did a time ever come when Thomas got along with his family?

A time came when he got along with himself. First, he had to ask: *Why do I believe my parent's opinion of me when I doubt their opinions on everything else?*

What did Thomas gain from coming here this lifetime?

Whatever emotion he gained along the way.

Did he continue doubting throughout his life?

Yes, but his doubts became more instinctive. *Why would Jesus be the only savior amongst us? Who are all the rest of us if he was God and we aren't?*

Many times during his life, Thomas heard me say that love was a choice. As a choice, it was available to everyone. Believing that was true, he put his determination behind the goal of always choosing love. When his journey ended, the illusion stayed behind, but the essence in him knew its meaning forever.

What did Thomas think would happen when he died?

He thought he would go on living. He believed that eternal life was a given–even if eternal use of a body was not. But he knew that I had lived the eternal use of mine. He wanted to know why. While it's true that I had a mind full of love toward the end of my journey, it wasn't a righteous kind of love, it was a kind of love where all were accepted as the same deliberate energy.

A mind full of love created a body full of love. Together, a mind and body full of love created wholeness. Wholeness enabled me to sense the heart of God wherever I was. Thomas kept this vision in front of him as he carried forth in life.

Thomas had the advantage of knowing you personally.

All souls created the advantages they believed would further their enlightenment.

But didn't you show Thomas that ascension was possible?

I proved that living in wholeness was the act of loving self.

Did every soul around you love itself completely?

No, but all who joined the heaven of eternal bliss did.

How did they find that bliss?

The same way Thomas found his: by remembering that the journey was emotional. When he opened to the beauty of every path, the insight of every soul, and the ecstasy of every gift, the love of God was his.

Did Thomas believe that God loved everyone equally?

Not always, but his heart was beautiful however it felt.

What kind of God accepted every feeling?

A God who held them all.

Did Thomas judge his past in negative ways?

Until he saw how the past had led to the present.

Maybe he only reacted badly when driven beyond his coping skills.

Maybe he only got driven beyond his coping skills when driving others beyond theirs. To take the sting out of backlash, Thomas had to see his reflection. Then he could say, *Well, what do you know! There's my mirror, steadfast and true as always.*

Did he cause accidents by losing control?

Accidents of like nature, but regardless of how he defined the nature of an accident, action/reaction prevailed. The good news was that once he knew it did, he could use that knowledge effectively. When he ignored action/reaction, reactions grew bolder. He could call that boldness being pushed beyond his coping skills, but to God, it was a gift moving him onward and inward.

Was Thomas greatly challenged in this lifetime?

He thought so, especially when he lost his wife. Granted, she didn't die to create pain for him, but he still felt bereft of her love. When he came to me in mourning, we had the following conversation:

Would you still feel bereft of her love if she was only traveling for a while? I asked him.

Not unduly, he said, *but I'd miss her physical presence.*

What if energy leaves the human plane for the same reason it travels; to expand its loving awareness? Could you be happy she was doing so?

Yes, he said, *but I still have to cope with the loss.*

Not if there is none. Energy in expansion has more of itself to share with you. More to the point, why are you sad at the possibility that she's expanding her awareness, but not sad at the possibility that she's visiting other places?

Because, he said, *if she's visiting other places, she'll return and we'll be together*.

Could you be happy with her destiny if a reunion was inevitable?

Yes, Thomas replied.

Wonderful, I said. Pretty soon, your loss will become a gain.

When Thomas got depressed and couldn't cope, did he take it out on others?

Yes; it evidenced as mocking laughter to hide the pain he felt. But to learn to cope, he had to put himself in the position of other people.

Was he honest about his setbacks?

He was honest about them after he did for himself what he wished others would do for him: accept him for who he was and what he had to offer.

Didn't that leave him feeling needy?

No, it got him what he needed–a mind out of negative doubt.

How could Thomas find more happiness if no one ever fulfilled him?

How could Thomas find more happiness while seeking the impossible? Happiness was the by-product of taking care of himself, not waiting for others to care-take.

Thomas was sure that if kinder people were around him, he'd be a happier person. I urged him to find those kinder people as quickly as possible, but he and I didn't always agree on how to do that.

Kindness and love were synonymous, weren't they?

We agreed on that.

They should be people who were respectful.

Yes, and I told Thomas they would be as soon as he was.

They needed to be people who were valuable.

Yes, and I assured him that everyone fit that description. He didn't agree. Then I suggested that perhaps he hadn't looked deep enough into his own heart to find that worthy reflection. *Approach the problem differently,* I said, *and instead of insisting that people give you what you need, give them what they need. Then you'll find your mirror.*

WHAT YOU FEEL IS WHAT YOU HAVE PRIORITIZED. THERE IS NO OTHER SECRET TO THE MEANING OF LIFE.

Worksheet Section:

Chapter 11 – Truth

Who is supposed to fulfill your needs?

How are they supposed to do it?

How would you feel if you thought you couldn't reach your potential without the support of others?

How would you like to feel instead?

What action can you take to get the feeling you want?

Questions to Ponder:

- *Am I teaching others to express themselves or teaching them to be mute?*
- *Am I helping others to serve their instincts, or to serve the monster called fear?*
- *Am I opening doors to encourage freedom or working to block more breakaways?*

HOW CAN YOU BE SURE THAT HAPPINESS IS POSSIBLE WHILE BELIEVING IT DEPENDS ON OTHERS?

Personal Insights

Blame is destructive, Jesus, *because it returns to you with the added power of physics.* I didn't understand this boomerang as a young girl, or even as I matured. Well into my forties, I still believed that others had to change before I could heal my heart. When Jesus said that no amount of periphery, or anything outside of me, would get me what I wanted, I was angry. How unfair, I thought. I'm the wronged party. *Sorry,* he said, *life isn't meant to be fair; it's meant to be informative.* And informative it is. Now the power has shifted. Instead of avoiding responsibility, I claim my autonomy and gladly take the helm. And to tell you the truth, being a pilot is a lot more fun than being a passenger.

CHAPTER 12

Advice

Whose advice is worthy?

TRUST THAT YOU ARE EVERYTHING YOU NEED TO BE.
TRUST THAT LIFE HAS MEANING.
TRUST THAT GOALS HAVE PURPOSE.
TRUST THAT "BEING" IS ENOUGH.

What kind of advice was worthy of giving to others, Jesus?
The kind I loved receiving.

With whom did you exchange advice?
Often, my friend, Lazarus.

The Lazarus who rose from the dead?
The Lazarus who elevated his mind to control his body.

Did he learn that from you?
He learned it from recognizing the oneness we shared.

Didn't you cause his resurrection?
No, Lazarus resurrected because he listened to himself and followed his heart.

How did he find that trust?
From being.

Wasn't it idealistic to believe that being was enough?
Yes, but ideals were all he had to work with. His body was also an ideal within his soul. If his ideals didn't enlighten him

this time around, he chose differently once he came again.

Didn't God bring Lazarus forth into humanness?

Yes, but the God who brought him forth was the God within himself. No other God had the relevant information. Only he knew what he needed to live in order to heal the part of his heart not yet inclusive.

Did Lazarus ever get stuck in painful ideals?

Yes, he got stuck when he demonized his father for the beatings he inflicted. For Lazarus to get unstuck, he had to ask the question that loosened the glue: *How have I pasted myself to the person in front of me by expressing similar emotions?*

How could an innocent child deserve abuse?

Lazarus didn't take an ideal to suffer; he took an ideal to eliminate suffering. He wanted to stop the cruel behavior that marked his previous journey, so he lived the personification of what it meant to receive it.

It may seem harsh to you that Lazarus chose to have a sadistic father, but in the big picture of his evolution, it was a lot less brutal than having lifetime after lifetime without any resolution.

Even if he had to live that resolution as a young and innocent child?

His energy was eternal; when it sensed a way to expand, it took the relevant path.

As an infant, how could Lazarus counter with love?

As an infant he didn't have to; his infant consciousness knew love was everywhere, in everyone and everything.

Did Lazarus prove that emotional action/reaction worked?

After he realized that proof was something he gave to himself, he did. The universe reciprocated quickly and efficiently. If he gave love, he got love. If he didn't, he got the something else he gave instead.

Would his father have been kinder had kinder people been with him?

Had his father been receptive to that kindness, yes, but all the kindness in the world couldn't change his father if his father wasn't ready to feel it. And to be ready to feel it, he had to be ready to give it.

How could Lazarus be of service to a father who was abusive?

By being the person he wished his father would be.

Why did Lazarus choose a lifetime in which he was less fortunate?

Why would Lazarus be less fortunate for taking a path with answers?

Did he struggle with other people besides his father?

He and I struggled, as each of us gave advice to the other that hadn't been asked for and wasn't seen as helpful. Then the one who gave it expected gratitude, while the one who received it saw nothing to be grateful for. Therefore, instead of getting the thanks we wanted we got rejected. But how could either of us enjoy advice that came to us unsolicited? Unsolicited advice was not a gift; it was a distraction.

Are you saying that you offered people unsolicited advice?

If I hadn't, I wouldn't have been so annoyed when Lazarus offered me his.

Was Lazarus a logical thinker?

Not always; the depth of his sadness often overwhelmed him. Then his mirror showed up: people capable of choosing happiness, but choosing sadness instead.

Are you saying that he knew how to improve his mood, but didn't take that action?

I'm saying that most people suffered this affliction. After all, if he had the power to reinforce sadness, he had the power to reinforce happiness.

Had his situation been different, would his attitude have been different?

His situation was different when his attitude changed.

If Lazarus had an idea to do something, wasn't that a fact not an attitude?

If Lazarus had an attitude that made life awful, it didn't matter what the facts were; the experience felt the same.

When else did you and Lazarus clash?

When I forgot that he had instincts to lead him wisely, too. Often I rattled on and on trying to convince him to take my advice, sure that if he did, he would avoid unnecessary risks.

However, that's what Lazarus did when he listened to me instead of himself. In fact, this was his predicament when he wanted to buy a house. Naturally, his instincts led him to the perfect home for him. Everything went smoothly until I intervened.

It's barely livable I told him, *and drainage problems have been a constant worry.* But he wasn't the owner when the drainage problems were happening. Had he become the owner, the house would then reflect his patterns, not the previous owner's.

Are you saying that a flooded house reflected an owner that didn't belong there?

I'm saying that a flooded house reflected an emotional issue the owner wanted to learn through.

What were those drainage problems about?

They represented water entering a space in which it did not belong; thereby affecting another space disadvantageously; the owner's dilemma exactly. He was borrowing money to maintain his standard of living. Therefore, he was occupying a space that drained him of his resources, or occupying a space in which he did not belong. Thus the water entered where it, too, did not belong.

When it came to whether Lazarus should live there, he only had to ask if he could afford to. If he could, the water would then reroute to where it belonged to reflect that he belonged where he was.

If life really worked this way, it was incredible.

Incredibly wonderful when Lazarus knew how to make it work for him.

Did the house have any other problems?

A house that was owned through excessive borrowing was likely to have quite a few. Lazarus only had to ask if he could work within that framework. My interference was more than Lazarus could handle and he didn't make the purchase. He called it a setback, but nothing was a setback if it woke him up to his instincts. If the pusher was someone he loved all the better. Powerful challenges created powerful miracles.

Did Lazarus have another relationship in which he was badly hurt?

He had a relationship in which he decided to feel hurt. His wife, Rachel, left him. Alone and miserable, he decided he didn't like it… that is, until he decided he did like it.

How could he arbitrarily decide to like it?

Why not? He had arbitrarily decided the opposite. Simple deduction told him that if **not** liking the situation had turned him into a lonely, frustrated, miserable man, liking it would be an improvement.

Did Rachel leave Lazarus with lots of responsibility?

If you call three children lots of responsibility, but instead of admitting the role he'd played in this drama, he blamed Rachel for all his woes and regrets.

Didn't she have obligations to him and the children?

Yes, and what do you think her obligations should have included?

Respect, consideration, and mothering.

What if Lazarus had all the mothering he needed, both for him and for his children, and to gain Rachel's respect, he had to admit it.

But did he have her mothering?

No, but he had enough mothering. More importantly, she had something else to offer in terms of his evolution.

What good was something else if she couldn't offer mothering?

What good was mothering if she had something else to offer? Expecting the impossible was to keep the problem alive. What she had to offer was the issue, not what she didn't have to offer.

If Rachel was absent, what could she offer?

Perhaps the gift of her absence. She offered Lazarus the gift he was ready to live, even if she didn't realize it and he didn't accept it. Lazarus didn't welcome the challenge when it arrived, but after he opened his heart to what he could learn from living it, miracles began.

Wasn't a miracle defined by something impossible happening?

That was one definition, and Lazarus thought it was impossible to find anything good in this situation. Therefore, it was a miracle when he did. Rachel didn't play the role he expected her to, but the children couldn't become contented adults from what their mother did or didn't do, only from what they did or didn't do.

After Rachael left, Lazarus told the children to hate her. Then they felt embittered. When Lazarus urged the children to love Rachel, even if they didn't see why they should, life improved for all of them.

If the children forgave their mother, didn't that make them even more vulnerable to abuse?

As the children forgave her, they attracted unconditional love back.

What happened when Lazarus told the children to hate?

He thwarted their natural instincts. When he released his judgment, the children received the greatest gift there was: proof that sadness and cynicism were emotions they could either accept or reject.

The Bible says an eye for an eye. Therefore, Rachel should have suffered for the suffering she caused her children.

What if an eye for an eye meant that Rachel's children would meet revenge in others if they lived a lot of their own?

Why would God punish innocent children?

God could only give these children the love they gave to others.

Did Rachel need to change?

Lazarus thought so but nothing improved until he dealt with

his own agenda instead of worrying about hers. The children followed suit and sadness left their lives.

Then Rachel had the best of both worlds. She left Lazarus but still had his love.

As he gave her the best of both worlds, God was able to give him the same. After all, God said an eye for an eye.

But then she had everything: the children's love, his love, and all the love in her new life. Where did that leave Lazarus?

Feeling very loved. Whatever he gave, God was able to give to him. He came to trust this theory by comparing the results he had when using it, to the results he had when not. Eventually he realized that each and every problem reflected an aspect of his life in which he refused to grow.

Did you help Lazarus to solve any problems?

Later in life I did, mostly through example. After returning from solitude, my ministry expanded. People who had previously attended Temple were now attending me. The rabbi, seeing the empty seats, began to look for allies. Lazarus was targeted.

Choose between us, the rabbi said to Lazarus, *allegiance to Jesus or allegiance to me.* Lazarus was aghast. The rabbi, in light of his weakening influence, was unmoved. Unable to make that choice, Lazarus retreated from both.

Exile didn't suit him and he mended fences quickly, at least with me. He tried to heal with the rabbi but the rabbi had conditions that Lazarus wouldn't accept. Nevertheless, regardless of those conditions, the rabbi and Lazarus shared a common dilemma. Lazarus was telling Rachel what the rabbi was telling him: who she had to be to regain his favor.

Both were searching for love and both were forgetting where to find it: the rabbi in thinking that my influence diminished his; and Lazarus in thinking that Rachel's influence diminished his.

The rabbi had a choice when dealing with Lazarus; Lazarus had a choice when dealing with Rachel. Both could say, *Find your happiness and live your life to the fullest,* or both could say, *Do as management deems wise or be damned.* But any position they took came back to them as well.

Did the rabbi suffer from Lazarus' defection?

He suffered when he told himself that defection was a suffering event. He wanted to be proven right in his beliefs, and thought if Lazarus were proven wrong in his, he would be. The rabbi's pressure took its toll and Lazarus came to me.

What do you want out of life, I asked him.

I want to hear your truths because they feel so much like mine.

Follow your heart, I said, *even the rabbi is trying to follow his.*

The issues that Lazarus had with the rabbi were never fully resolved, but Lazarus found peace from following his heart, at least temporarily.

Why only temporarily?

Because peace was impossible while believing that I had help in ways that he did not. In fact, his digression over this issue reached the point where his unconscious had to take over in order to wake him up. Dramatic though it was, through the illusion of death, his soul had to be outrageousness to get the mind's attention. It began with an illness so severe, he only had time to say *Find Jesus*. When I returned and found his body, I spoke to him as I had so many times before: *Your body follows wherever the mind takes it, so love the journey, appreciate the gift, and value the growth it offered. There will never be another experience exactly like this one. Honor your choices and believe in what they taught you.*

Out-of-body, the logic in Lazarus instantly took over. He realized that he and I were the same love of God, equal in beauty and equal in support. As he brought this truth to his body, it merged with the soul in oneness–and he was back enjoying both.

Was that a miracle?

It was a thought transformation. Lazarus resurrected from acting on his knowledge of oneness, exactly the way he had acted on his knowledge when birthing into his body. Granted, he *re-entered* his older body this time, but he re-entered it for the same reason he entered his young body at birth: for the love it could offer his soul.

What did his body tell him as it lay dead and useless?

Nothing, but the love in his soul told him that the body would embrace whatever use he gave it. As Lazarus believed in the beauty of this love, oneness of body and soul were his.

Did he enjoy this union for the rest of his human journey?

Each time he loved in the face of reasons not to, he did.

MAKE SURE YOU DON'T CHEAT, HARASS, DISRESPECT, INSULT, OR ANTAGONIZE YOURSELF, BY MAKING SURE YOU DON'T DO IT TO OTHERS.

Worksheet Section:

Chapter 12 – Advice

Who gives you unsolicited advice?

Has it helped you to become a happier, more compassionate person?

If it hasn't, why are you still listening?

What do you want to hear instead?

How can you give that news to others?

Questions to Ponder:

- *Am I running from something unpleasant or moving toward something productive?*
- *Am I anticipating more dependency or anticipating more freedom?*
- *Am I thinking that life has limits, or that life has limitless possibilities?*

**BELIEVE IN YOUR WISDOM
IF YOU WANT TO GET RID OF FEAR.
WHEN THIS DISRUPTER IS GONE,
LIFE IS SEEN AS DEAR.**

Personal Insights:

I find it hard to trust advice. Not because it isn't sound, but because it's often generic. What is helpful to another might not be helpful to me. I trust an inner voice that I refer to as my instincts. However, one caveat must be noted. I have to feel the love in this voice before I can trust its message. Another voice is trying to be heard and often sounds convincing. It has a different focus, however, on things, events, and people, or what is happening outside of me instead of within my heart.

To know if love is speaking, I have to remember that love doesn't judge what is right or wrong, good or bad, or more or less important. Love has a solution that works for everyone. Those who helped me to trust this voice were the people who offered the biggest challenges; and the reason they were so helpful was because they forced me to live what I otherwise would not have. Some of these people turned out to be wonderful friends; some did not. But I honor them all equally because each and every one of them participated in my evolution. And for that I will always be grateful.

CHAPTER 13

Complaints

How do complaints affect us?

WELCOME WHAT IS AND WHAT WAS, THEN WHAT COMES FEELS WELCOMED.

Did anyone ever complain about you, Jesus?

Andrew complained about me when my less than magical fishing skills appeared. As a volunteer to replace disabled fishermen, I was enthusiastic at first. After the boats were launched, and Andrew's memory of my inadequacies would return, I felt like a liability. By then, however, it was too late to do anything about it.

Andrew never lost any men because of my inability to perform like a seasoned sailor, but we never got home without a lot of critiques on his part and a lot of sorry's on mine. He felt badly about his complaining and always apologized, reassuring me that I had carried my weight. I knew differently. My skills were minimal and everyone knew it.

Was it fair to critique you when you were only trying to help?

It was fair to expect the best from me that I could possibly offer. It's just that the best I had to offer was no where near the best that Andrew could offer. It was the best of a preaching carpenter whose skills were clearly elsewhere.

Did you feel awful when you felt Andrew's displeasure?

Had I minimized the skills of someone else, I did.

Did Andrew and Peter fish together?

Yes, they were brothers in a family business.

Did Andrew complain to Peter about you?

No, but he complained to Peter about Peter, saying that Peter's moods could sure use improvement when he was out on the water. Peter told Andrew to set a better example and maybe he'd follow suit. Andrew accepted the challenge and demonstrated that a good catch was incidental to the good time had while catching.

Did Andrew choose to be a fisherman before he came into humanness?

Before he came into humanness, he hoped to love whatever he chose. Fishing was the relevant choice for most of his active life. During his many adventures, he discovered that regardless of what he was doing or where he was, the light he shone on others was the light shone back on him.

Are you referring to the meting out of fair and appropriate punishment/reward?

Justice didn't function within the framework of punishment. Justice read his aura and acted on his own behalf to bring his mirror back. Andrew didn't always appreciate the abundance he attracted, but it still returned and it still remained appropriate.

Wasn't abundance all the good stuff?

Abundance was whatever was. He determined the stuffing ingredients.

Andrew deserved to be loved, didn't he?

He deserved whatever he thought others deserved.

Why should Andrew love those who weren't deserving?

So that he could get what he deserved.

Regardless of whom he faced?

Since he only faced himself, yes. Procrastination was not effective in a world run by physics. If Andrew looked in the mirror, what could the mirror reflect from thought alone?

Nothing, but if Andrew spoke a lot, his mouth moved around a lot.

If that was the only action taken, that was the only action begotten. Mirrors couldn't philosophize; they could only reflect. Andrew could tell his mirror all manner of things and, still, it only gave him who he was.

Did Andrew live these physics with someone besides Peter?

He lived them with his father, Jona. Andrew saw his father as having a mouth that rarely stopped and a mind that rarely followed.

Be brave, respect yourself, make your mark, chart your plans, carry through, and never steal, is what Jona said. What he lived was something else, cowering before his superiors, caving in under pressure, and taking what he wanted paid for or not. Jona's hypocrisy turned Jona into a man who wasn't likable; therefore, Andrew did the opposite in order to like himself.

Couldn't Andrew tell the difference between good and bad advice?

He could tell the difference between what his father said to do and what his father did. Andrew followed his father's behavior not his father's words. Then Jona became more aggressive in his effort to be obeyed.

Jona saw himself as a patriarch, managing kin and subordinates. He didn't realize that his own autonomy suffered as he denied others theirs. *I'm not self-destructive,* he thought. *Surely others are crueler to me than I'm capable of being to myself.*

As Andrew matured, he turned into his father, preaching about a godly way to live, and doing the opposite.

Why didn't Jona change his tactics when he realized they weren't working?

He wanted to, but he couldn't see himself as a free agent while telling others they weren't. The universe interpreted *I want to dominate* into *I want to be dominated.* After Andrew saw himself in his father, he began to heal; not because his father stopped being a tyrant, but because Andrew recognized the tyrant in himself.

Did he believe in the theory of emotional action/reaction?

Not until he tested it to prove it worked for him. Even my enthusiasm wasn't enough to convince him; after all, he'd heard many of my theories throughout the years; some I had kept, some I had not.

After Andrew believed in action/reaction, did anyone try to dissuade him from his beliefs?

Yes, but after he'd lived action/reaction to understand its properties, no one could tell him it didn't work.

Did Jona's tyranny have any lasting benefits?

Andrew thought so or he wouldn't have been his son. He could learn from that hostility, or, he could curse the world and everyone in it. As a youngster he did the latter, complaining about his father on a fairly regular basis.

As a child, wasn't it expecting too much for Andrew to understand a domineering parent?

As an adult, was it expecting too much to understand his father?

As an adult, Andrew had other people to turn to.

And what if he turned to those who continued to feed the sympathy syndrome?

Then he had to look further for those who didn't.

Then why couldn't he look further in his youth?

Because his confidence level was lower in his youth.

If his confidence level was low in his youth, why would it be higher later?

Because his confidence would grow as he matured, wouldn't it?

Not necessarily. Maturity was an inner process not an outer process. The longer Andrew stayed in unproductive patterns, the harder they were to break. Experience had no advantage if it didn't seed independence.

Maybe he was in pain.

Maybe he was. And if so, wouldn't he seek relief?

Yes, but why would he find it later if he couldn't find it sooner?

Because his need for relief intensified; Andrew wanted a father he could respect. He tried everything he could think of to create that kind of bond. Neither his irrational rage nor fawning kindness created the bond he wanted. Friends interceded, reminding him of the pressure Jona was under.

Knowing it was true, Andrew made a concerted effort to be the person he hoped his father would be. His new congeniality attracted many pleasant responses, but neither his niceness nor his rebelliousness impacted with his father.

Angered by that indifference, Andrew forgot the reason he needed to love: not so that Jona's life would improve, but so that his own life would improve.

Did Jona like Andrew?

Andrew didn't think so, but whether Jona liked him or not was irrelevant. He had to appreciate the people who *did* like him and forget about those who didn't. Andrew wanted a feeling from Jona that Jona didn't have. And wanting something from Jona that Jona didn't have, was a problem Andrew had, not a problem Jona had.

Eventually, Andrew saw the humor in his predicament: he was so preoccupied with complaining about Jona's behavior that he forgot to notice his own.

When all this was happening, were you preaching to do unto others as they wanted to be done to?

Yes, and I was preaching the difference between living this theory and speaking it, or, the difference between a happy existence and one that was filled with hate, disease, and heartache. To do unto others was not the same as to talk unto others. Doing was active. Therefore, if Andrew wanted an emotion done to him, he had to do that emotion to others. A bunch of words wouldn't produce regardless of how many he used or what the dictionary said they meant.

When Andrew complained that nothing was working and he was stuck, I reminded him that to walk through illusion successfully, he had to understand the difference between illusion and reality. When Andrew was confused, we had the following conversation:

To know what is real, I said, you have to know what is unreal, or, the nature of illusion.

Okay, Andrew responded, *illusion looks real but isn't.*

Does today seem real? I asked him.

Yes.

And what about tomorrow, does that seem real?

Not yet. It's still a possibility.

What about yesterday? Is that real?

It happened. Now it's just a memory.

You believe in yesterday because you remember living it. You believe in tomorrow because today is here and you have a memory of yesterday. If you hadn't lived yesterday, and tomorrow never came, how would you view the moment?

As everything, he replied.

Before the mind of God conceived of a yesterday and a tomorrow, it lived the only reality it had: the moment. In order to live the un-real, it had to create an illusion in which to live it. That's what yesterday and tomorrow are: apparitions devised so energy can live the dimension of *time.*

Tell me again why yesterday wasn't real, he said.

It was real when you lived it. Now it's just a memory.

But I experienced it.

What did you experience?

Activities, people, jobs, things like that.

What do you remember the most about those activities, people, and jobs?

How I felt about them.

Exactly; anything strongly felt is still with you, anything not is gone. If you have an emotion today, chances are it will still be with you tomorrow. Ten years from now, you'll be enjoying the moment, plus all your pleasing memories. That's why energy invests in time. It's a way of building on joyous reservoirs. Do you like the possibility that you're here to enhance the treasure of love within?

Yes, but sometimes the opposite happens.

Only because you forget what *you're* here to find and build on something else. Nothing on the outside has validity unless it inspires love. To evaluate for meaningful truth, evaluate your eternal self. What you see with your eyes cannot support your journey. *It's* a dream affecting the heart so the source can be revealed.

What happened when Andrew healed?

He wanted to share his healing. And here is his message to each and every one of you:

Dear friends,

Take my hand as you wander through your day. Not so that I can show you any wonders in my world, but so that you can show me the wonders in yours. I too had a curious mind as I challenged the status quo. Many times I did so with my hands and what they could touch. Many times I did so with my soul and what I could feel. But, always, I was looking for new frontiers and ways to engage the intangible. What a miracle you have before you! What creativity you have brought to this heavenly game! I am deeply moved by the depth to which you have stretched your unlimited souls; so broad are your innovations, so great are your commitments, so deep are your imaginings. No effort has ever been wasted, no beginning ever forgotten, and no accomplishment ever lost. Now and forever you are the light you shine, the love you share, and the beauty you bestow.

**ABUNDANCE IS SELF-INSPIRED.
REMEMBER THIS WHEN YOU THINK
THAT SOMEONE ELSE
IS THE SOURCE OF WHAT YOU NEED.**

Worksheet Section:

Chapter 13 – Complaints

When did you last complain?

Did you complain from a need to heal within or from a need to change another?

Was either accomplished?

Do you want the feeling of accomplishment?

Then admire the people around you and make sure they know how you feel.

Questions to Ponder:

- *Do I inspire self-revelation or self-reviling?*
- *Do I love myself, or do I try to get others to love me?*
- *Do I discipline myself to love, or do I discourage the presence of discipline?*

**CHERISH THE PROCESS.
YOU NEVER LEAVE IT BEHIND YOU.
YOU SIMPLY BRING MORE OF YOURSELF
TO THE PROCESS YOU ARE IN.**

Personal Insights

If Jesus is right and illusion isn't real, what does that mean? I imagine my future; I even imagine the people who might be in it. Some of them aren't real yet, but they will be.

When I asked Jesus about this, he said, *Why is the future so important? Isn't it because you think it will bring you love?* Yes, I said. *So if love is in the moment and you're happy now, why does it matter what the future brings?* It does because the future will have the picture I need. *Pictures don't hold emotion,* he responded. *Hearts hold emotion. Needs are emotional. The moment is everything. Today is the sum total of who you are. To gain more of who you are is a mental discipline. Therefore, if you see the emotional goodness of now, you'll be seeing it in the future as well.*

CHAPTER 14

Acceptance

Is acceptance necessary?

YOU CAN CHOOSE TO SEE THE LOVE IN YOUR LIFE OR YOU CAN CHOOSE TO SEE THE OPPOSITE. BUT IF YOU HAVE A CHOICE, WHY NOT SEE THE LOVE?

Did the people you knew eventually become more accepting?

Every soul believed it would and came here trying to prove it.

Even when others were cruel?

Especially when others were cruel. Who needed acceptance when the world was full of love? When it wasn't, that's when acceptance counted.

Did you know anyone who struggled to be accepted?

My friend Thaddeus struggled to be accepted. As a child with a stutter, he not only had the shame of family to cope with, but also the frustration of doctors and the ridicule of peers. As he grew into puberty, his body matured attractively and confidence grew. The stuttering abated until he had to earn a living. Then it returned with a vengeance.

His father, hoping to jumpstart his career, resorted to nepotism to make it happen. Thaddeus knew he was in trouble the first day on the job. Instead of feeling welcomed, he felt resented. As fellow workers ignored him, he went to his father and asked him to intervene. His father, equally challenged to get along with co-workers, wasn't much help.

Frustrated, Thaddeus spoke unkindly about his father, hoping to be seen as separate from him and therefore, apart from the problem. Instead he was seen as ungrateful.

Confused and naïve regarding office politics, he volunteered for extra hours, hoping that hard work and persistence would get him through this crisis.

Judas, another employee, convinced that he would have had that job had his talents been fairly rewarded, noted Thaddeus' incompetence every chance he got, not only to his face but also behind his back. Unprepared for Judas' anger, Thaddeus tried to avoid him. But no amount of avoidance could keep the pain away. As the weight of judgment burdened his self-esteem, the stuttering took its toll.

When he came to me for guidance, I softened the blow by reassuring Thaddeus that Judas only behaved as he did from a need to feel appreciated. I also told him that if Judas hoped to feel more secure by making him feel less secure, Judas was in for a big shock. And perhaps Thaddeus should be there to support Judas when that happened.

He asked me why he should support a man who treated him so badly. *Why else,* I said, *to help you avoid that non-support in the future. After all, Judas only did to you what you did to your father: speak unkindly about you behind your back.*

Did Thaddeus make excuses?

He spoke of a voice inside him predicting zero talent, and ridiculing his every effort to connect with the people around him. Then, he'd stammer, sweat, get red in the face, and lose any sense of composure.

I told him that I couldn't heal the stutter for him; I could only urge him to focus on his strengths instead of his weaknesses. Thaddeus did as I suggested and gained a positive focus. Then, instead of fretting over his flaws, he started appreciating his assets. As faith in himself grew, he was able to tolerate occasional teasing and sometimes even return it.

Did Judas and Thaddeus ever become good friends?

No, Judas was unwilling. Thaddeus, however, came to the conclusion that his father was only trying to help him. From insight he found grace. Then he was able to admit that, if he was only searching for acceptance as he attacked his father, the same must be true of Judas.

What could Judas have done differently?

Whatever he hoped would be done for him. Would he have hassled Thaddeus had he known he was really only hassling himself?

Did Thaddeus stay in the job and eventually get accepted?

He stayed in the job and eventually accepted himself. Co-workers sensed his resolve to overcome his shortcomings, and saw more reasons to overcome theirs.

As an adult, how was Thaddeus seen by other people?

As an attractive man, shy and rather introverted. But their perception had little to do with his. He still found it difficult to counteract the voice inside attacking his self-image. He blamed his inability to turn things around on his introverted nature.

I responded by asking him, *What is wrong with silence. What is wrong with shyness? What is wrong with reserve? You only make them wrong because you don't feel accepted. And you think that a smart, witty, and erudite personality* ***will*** *be accepted.*

Participation was not the problem for Thaddeus; participating in comfort was. He couldn't relax while listening to a voice that said: *Talk if you want to be somebody, joke if you want to be noticed, orate if you want to be loved.* The worst aspect of shyness was the feeling of not being seen. He only wanted to belong.

Didn't Thaddeus attract other shy people to him?

Yes, but as he acted aggressively against his nature, dichotomy came back. Then it was two uncomfortably shy people trying to be who they weren't. Only after he accepted himself and rejoiced in his many attributes did he attract the same deliverance.

Did he appreciate having you around, Jesus?

He appreciated having an objective listener. Ironically, I was part of the problem in his youth. Thaddeus' father, insecure in his own conviviality, wanted a son who could talk, mingle, and articulate–not an invisible no-show. When it became obvious that Thaddeus was the latter, his father took to muttering under his breath, *Why can't you be more like Jesus?* Unable to verbalize the pain of that rejection, Thaddeus internalized it.

But the pain didn't disappear; it just expressed differently, and once it manifested, there was no possibility that he could become his father's ideal.

What did Thaddeus hope would happen to improve his life?

He hoped that someone would come along and give him the one gift to improve it. I suggested that he give that gift to himself because, then, he could stop worrying if that other person would ever show up.

Did Thaddeus live any miracles?

He was the miracle. He only had to love that it was so.

I thought miracles were thought transformations.

That's what he was. His soul imagined him; as the power of that inspiration grew, the dream made manifest.

Did Thaddeus plan his journey by himself?

He planned it with those who embraced similar challenges.

When he remembered that oneness, he unmasked more of the miracle within.

How did he come to know this part of himself?

By existing. *Being* was the ultimate.

But Thaddeus wasn't living the ultimate.

If he hadn't been, he wouldn't have been here.

Are you saying that all your friends were living the ultimate just because they were here?

If there was anything wiser for them to experience, they would have been doing so.

Did Thaddeus live long enough to find the growth he aspired to?

He aspired to love. When he found it, time disappeared. And since *time* was a tool to help him find what was real, and reality was love, he only had to remember the meaning of time and use it well.

Even if Thaddeus loved his life, didn't his body continue to age as each day ended?

Each day ended as the Earth spun in its orbit and the sun was hidden from view. What did that have to do with aging?

It was something he saw with his eyes.

Had he been blind, how would he have known that aging had occurred?

He would have felt less youthful and had less stamina.

What if he only lost his stamina from believing in his yesterdays and thinking the body should age?

Didn't everyone think time and aging went together?

There were some who believed differently. Naturally, they were with others in the same belief.

Was it hard for Thaddeus to imagine not aging?

No harder than it was to imagine people aging differently. He knew that hard times created stress, and stress caused aging. From that deduction, he decided that a lack of stress could curtail the aging process.

Completely?

If the ease was complete.

Wasn't that a radical thought?

Perhaps, but he didn't think it was radical that a lack of stress prolonged a person's youth. And once a belief was embraced, it then became the consensus.

How was Thaddeus supposed to create comfort in the presence of hate and cruelty?

Believe it or not, that's where the *most* love was waiting. To find it, he only had to open his heart; release, forgive, and move on.

Did you ever stop aging, Jesus?

Yes. Then I demonstrated my skill by sharing *the art of being*.

Weren't you doing all sorts of nice things for others?

That was God just being. I spoke of *God within his element* in as many ways as I could: one of them was the art of meditation. Thaddeus sensed my joy in participation and wanted the same for himself.

When he first began this practice, he thought of himself as an average man, fairly content, learning to love and accept himself.

As the meditation deepened, he thought of himself as a genius; a person who had brought the perfect exterior to explore the perfect interior. Eventually, he reached a depth so magnificent, it lifted him beyond the limitations of matter; and with a focus on the infinite, finite thought receded.

Finite thought as in aging?

While sitting in infinity, aging was a useless concept; he connected with his soul and felt eternal.

Didn't agelessness buck the world's consensus?

Yes, but it also bucked the world's consensus that someone could ascend. However, because I'd proven it possible, the idea grew. The concept of longer lives went through the same metamorphosis and eventually became the consensus. As old frontiers were accepted, new frontiers emerged to challenge the soul even deeper.

Did Thaddeus think of God as a he or a she?

He thought of God as both. If others didn't agree, they chose to please themselves. Love didn't expand from depicting the gender of God; it expanded from seeing the beauty in the gender God was.

Did Thaddeus trust that ascension would happen to him?

He trusted that his body reflected his current thought.

When it came to ascension, weren't there extra steps?

Extra steps referred to momentum. One loving thought became two, two loving thoughts became three, and so forth. Regardless of the energy ascending, the absolute laws of the universe prevailed. Thaddeus tested these physics to prove how well they worked. After that, the only thing left to remember was what he had already proven.

Was Thaddeus an intelligent man?

Intelligent enough for the healing of his heart. People often said he had everything he needed to live a productive life; still he doubted his assets. People praised his sweet and gentle nature; still he envied the dissidents. People hinted that a face like his could get him any women he wanted; still he felt insecure. People lauded his loyalty to me in the last few days of my life; still he felt neglectful.

Other opinions had little power to change his view of himself. He never dreamed of living an exemplary life, but he never stopped trying to. And much to his delight, when the final curtain fell, the play had completed itself with honor, dignity, and self-respect.

SEE GROWTH AND LIVE IN LIGHT.
SEE CRUELTY AND LIVE IN FRIGHT.
SEE HATRED THE SOUL DESCENDS.
SEE LOVE THE SOUL ASCENDS.

Worksheet Section:

Chapter 14 – Acceptance

What do you love about yourself and accept with ease?

Is that acceptance similar to your acceptance of others?

What do you dislike about yourself and wish were different?

Is that dislike similar to your dislike of others?

To heal, see everyone through the eyes of growth.

Questions to Ponder:

- *Do I prove my worthiness by what I think and speak, or by what I do and give?*
- *Do I honor my instincts and let them have their way, or do I doubt my instincts and let my fears have sway?*
- *Do I judge my every action and exist in negativity, or I do love my every action and exist in happy optimism?*

BEFORE YOU COME HERE,
YOUR AURA REFLECTS YOUR KARMA.
AFTER YOU LEAVE HERE,
YOUR AURA REFLECTS
HOW YOU DEALT WITH KARMA.

Personal Insights

My biggest challenge has been to love and accept myself. Why? Partly because of expectations, not only parental but personal as well. On many fronts, life didn't evolve as I'd been led to believe it would. Then I had to create new expectations outside the box of my upbringing. As I struggled with new demands, I blamed my pain on the actions of others. Much to my surprise, they turned out to be the miracles waiting to happen, for as I accepted them as the people they needed to be, I accepted myself as the person I needed to be. As I stopped blaming them for every setback, setbacks ceased to be. As I realized how strong I'd become from the challenge they had offered, I knew that anything making me stronger had to be viewed as valuable.

CHAPTER 15

Hearts

What constitutes a big heart?

**AUTONOMY IS THE GOAL.
THEREFORE,
WHATEVER COMPELS YOU TO LIVE IT
IS THE BIG IDEA YOU'RE AFTER.**

Was your heart in constant growth, Jesus?
Yes, although I didn't always believe it was.

What made you believe it?
The size of my heart when I saw it as my savior.

Are you saying that you were your own savior?
I'm saying that my heart was free to believe in the love it held.

Did you face many people whose hearts were growing like yours?
Yes, and one of them was Kaleb.

Was he a friend of yours?
Not in the sense that Peter, Andrew and Lazarus were friends, but moments after meeting, I recognized our oneness.

Did Kaleb recognize it, too?
He recognized that his healing was as close to him as his own loving instincts.

Did he ever ignore his instincts?
Sometimes, if he thought they were making someone else

suffer. But the voice that told him not to follow his instincts because so and so would suffer was the so and so that caused all his suffering.

Did Kaleb distinguish himself in some way?

He distinguished himself in business, at least in terms of outwardly seen success. However, an obsession with the picture to the exclusion of his heart created a mind out of sync with its purpose. A mind out of sync with its purpose created a body out of sync with its purpose. A body out of sync with its purpose had no reason for being. For Kaleb, that resulted in a heart condition by the age of twenty-five.

Tormented by the voice that said, *Nobody knows what they're doing; the world is going to pot; and the government gets crazier by the day,* he couldn't hear the voice that said, *People are as smart as they are loving, the world reflects its populace; and the government speaks for those who allow its presence.* As his body reacted to the content of his mind, he spent a fortune trying to heal it.

What did Kaleb hope to gain from doing well in business?

What everyone hoped to gain from a talent they enjoyed: a heart full of love and contentment. While planning his incarnation, he asked himself, *What can I bring to bless my journey, keep me focused, and honor my fellow travelers at the same time?* Once that path was established, choices were made to facilitate it. But the core idea was, and always would be, to fill his heart with love.

Did Kaleb's preoccupation with business prevent his heart from growing?

No, intellect was the problem bringing a sense of arrogance. Arrogance told him that he was a cut above others. To see himself as a cut above was to see others as a cut below. The cells received his message that inferiority was around, and reflected his attitude with a lot of inferior functioning. Cells couldn't reason the way the conscious mind could reason. They couldn't say to themselves, *Well, maybe he means that inferiority is only in this person and that person.* Cells were inclusive. Therefore, they accepted inferiority as the love in Kaleb's life.

When his health deteriorated and he couldn't physically search for healers, he had to wait for the shamans to come to him. Such an assortment arrived that his sense of humor vastly improved. In fact, he'd wake up in the morning and say to himself, *Well Kaleb, how many quacks will find their way to your doorstep today?*

Did Kaleb follow his doctor's instructions?

No, quite the opposite; he stubbornly refused to relinquish an iota of responsibility. Jeremiah, a long-time friend and physician, reached the end of his patience and told Kaleb that unless he stopped fussing over every detail, he'd kill himself. Kaleb said he'd rather die than surrender leadership. Knowing disaster would strike if Kaleb didn't relent, Jeremiah went to Kaleb's family and asked them to intervene. They refused to. Then he went to the staff and asked them to hide the work. They wouldn't. Then he threatened to summon me; a man Kaleb considered to be the biggest quack of them all.

Fine, Kaleb said, *summon Jesus. What difference does it make? I can't even sit up to eat a decent meal.* There he was, flat on his back, running an empire from a big old wooden bed.

I arrived and Kaleb didn't know what to make of me at first. No mention was made of his bed-ridden state. We conversed about his family, his politics, community issues; anything that seemed to hold his interest. We each had a point of view from which to communicate, and we each allowed the other to speak his thoughts.

Gradually, as Kaleb relaxed, I said to Jeremiah, *Kaleb sounds sane enough to me.* No argument there from Kaleb. As Jeremiah and I went into the next room to confer, I saw an expression on

Kaleb's face that told me he was wondering what in the world he had gotten himself in for this time. But no sooner had he pondered the question than I returned and said to him, *Well Kaleb, Jeremiah and I have discussed your case and concluded that you have the same thing wrong with you that we have wrong with us.*

Startled, he thought, *They have heart conditions too?* Then he looked into my eyes and knew exactly what I meant: We all come here with heart conditions and we're all trying to heal them. Seeing the humor in his drama, Kaleb said, *Well Jesus, if you're the same as me, you should be in bed.* I laughed and said, *Well Kaleb, if you're the same as me, you should be standing up.* He agreed and out of bed he got. To his amazement, he felt light as a feather and better than ever. Laughter, starting in his toes, traveled to the top of his head like a stream of creamy light, filling every pore of his being. His body felt weightless, his heart jubilant, and his mind ecstatic. He thanked me profusely. I told him that his ecstasy was all the thanks I needed.

Did Kaleb offer you money?

No, money didn't feel appropriate; the moment was already full of completion.

Did you know why Kaleb healed?

Yes, he had lived a lifetime of honoring his instincts, and so had I. He had delighted in his ambitions from the time he was old enough to have them, and so had I. He knew that life wasn't worth living if he couldn't do what he loved, and so did I. In the presence of that reflection, transformation was easy.

Did anyone doubt that Kaleb had healed?

It was pretty hard to doubt his health; he was up and around. Some doubted that he'd been sick in the first place, but Kaleb didn't care. He'd felt the transformation to know its properties.

Did his heart condition get him?

It got him all right, right into the heart of God forever.

Did Kaleb worry about backsliding?

Yes, and I told him he had a choice. He could remember the feeling of healing and reinforce it, or he could forget the feeling and reinforce something else.

Who would choose something else?

Whoever needed to test even more.

Who would be foolish enough to do that?

Everyone who has ever graced this planet. Kaleb arrived in the human game at one with the God within. After that, his future depended on the focus he took in the challenge he faced.

Did Kaleb's healing mark the end of his human journey?

It marked the end of his belief that he couldn't join the all-knowing force behind it.

Was his healing a resurrection?

Yes, but the process of resurrection was gradual. He found an idea he liked and he tested it. When he liked the results, he kept the idea and built on it. But it wasn't as if he was here one moment and gone the next; he was here one moment and everywhere the next. Every soul moved on to greater love, not always to body resurrection but to relevant resurrection.

Wasn't body resurrection the ultimate resurrection?

For those who desired bodily resurrection it was, but millions of souls in other wonderful dreams didn't look any less wise for their preference.

Did Kaleb want the resurrection that joined him to the whole of love?

Eventually, but until he saw the whole of love as desirable, he wasn't inclined to join it.

History doesn't speak of other resurrections that day.

History speaks of the love that was shared, and love was always the catalyst.

Did Kaleb have many obstacles to overcome this lifetime?

He had quite a few; he was born into a religion that dictated his moral code, a family that dictated his social code, and a government that dictated his political code. As he criticized these factions, he attracted critics back. As he rebutted those critics with acts of cruelty, acts of aggression reflected in his body.

Did Kaleb have greater obstacles to overcome than most people?

He thought so, but the greater the obstacle, the greater the revelation.

Did he think his money would bring him lots of love?

He hoped it would. When it didn't, he tried harder to make it happen. Then he got stuck in hopeless equations: *With my next completed building, I'll feel wealthy. With my next important tenant, I'll feel noticed. With my next prestigious deal, I'll feel accepted.*

As he tried to prove these premises, he pushed his body until it was literally sick of life and pushed others until they were literally sick of him. In terms of earning a living he was a master; in terms of honoring that master, a novice.

Did Kaleb want the approval of others?

Sometimes, but to feel that approval, he had to give that approval. He lived this lesson well with his daughter, Sarah. Headstrong like he was, she pushed to get her way as much as he pushed to get his. Kaleb didn't see her as his mirror, however, he saw her as his nemesis.

Maybe he worried that Sarah didn't know what she was doing?

Maybe he did, but to know what she was doing was to follow her heart.

Would their relationship have improved had he changed his philosophy?

Had he taken the one he wanted her to take, yes. The difference between the one he had and the one he needed was the difference between how Sarah treated him and how he wished she would.

Did God judge Kaleb for wanting to guide his daughter?

The question is, did Kaleb judge himself for ignoring her wisdom? He thought he was protecting Sarah, but Sarah wasn't asking for foolish freedoms; just for more control in her own environment. Kaleb told her she was making awful choices, but choices were only awful if the growth they wrought was ignored.

Sarah's goal was not to go through life making wonderful choices anyway; her goal was to go through life enjoying the choices made.

Wasn't it idealistic to hope for perfect harmony?

Perhaps but low expectations fulfilled themselves, too. He rationalized his decisions saying that his friends were making the same ones. But cause and effect, or action/reaction, didn't relate to patriarchal societies and the expectations around them; action/reaction related to emotion. Therefore, the consequences of every action still had to be handled.

Was Sarah compassionate toward her father in terms of his illness?

Yes, but compassion was not the issue; respect was. And since she received so little from him, she saw no reason to give it back.

Kaleb's problem was not a lack of love; it was a lack of understanding. Sarah wasn't averse to hearing his opinions; only to having hers negated in the process. To help her find her happiness, Kaleb had to help her achieve what she already knew was wise.

Was Kaleb's father alive while Kaleb was raising Sarah?

Yes but instead of urging Kaleb to love Sarah for her own sweet uniqueness, Isaac urged Kaleb to put the fear of God in her; the fear he'd put in Kaleb, of course. Kaleb resisted. He didn't want Sarah to suffer as he had. But the older he got and the bolder she got, the more he turned into his father.

Was Kaleb's father ambitious?

He had been in his youth. As an adult, Isaac abandoned his ambitions to fulfill his father's ambitions. When Kaleb came along, Isaac believed that if Kaleb didn't fulfill his yearnings, then he, as Kaleb's father, would feel better that he hadn't fulfilled his.

Neither Kaleb nor Isaac was intentionally cruel, but parental influences were well-seeded in their psyches. The good news was that healthy influences flourished as soon as the old ones were faced and dealt with.

Isaac's goal was honorable: to be a good parent; he just forgot the nature of good parenting. He got behind Kaleb when he thought his goals were suitable. When he didn't, he fought him every inch of the way. Then Kaleb did the same when it came to Sarah.

Did Isaac get to the point of feeling too old to enjoy his life?

He got to the point of using that excuse. Kaleb challenged him to find the good regardless. Isaac grudgingly admitted that he liked to talk to his neighbors, and he liked to look at the moon. Kaleb noticed, however, that as soon as Isaac's neighbors irritated him, he cut them out of his life.

In terms of his moon vigils, Isaac enjoyed them because they made him feel closer to God. Kaleb wondered how life would have treated Isaac had he dealt with his neighbors the way he dealt with his moon vigils. After all, if appreciation for the moon had made him feel closer to God, why wouldn't appreciation of his neighbors have done the same?

Maybe Isaac didn't like his neighbors the way they were.

Maybe he didn't, but if the moon hadn't been the moon he wanted it to be, would he have found such inspiration through it? Life had to be appreciated for how it was for the joy of life to be felt.

When Kaleb healed, did he feel that God had favored him over others?

Not in the least. Compare it to the process of consumption. Kaleb didn't think to himself, *lucky me; I'm enjoying what no one else can eat* because he knew that everyone had the same opportunity to eat whatever they pleased. Different foods were popular with different people, but those with similar tastes were together, consuming the food they loved.

ALL HAVE THE SAME OPPORTUNITY.
ALL HAVE THE SAME OPERANDI.
ALL DECIDE WHAT TO DO WITH IT.

Worksheet Section:

Chapter 15 - Hearts

What legacies were put upon you as a child?

What kind of a life did you yearn for instead?

Which of those dreams have been fulfilled?

Are you appreciating the dreams already completed?

What dreams do you have that still need more completion?

Questions to Ponder:

- *Am I willing to listen to others, or do I wait for others to listen to me?*
- *Am I open to other opinions or only seeking agreement?*
- *Am I sharing my heart willingly or forcing my will on others?*

**AT THE END OF THE JOURNEY,
EVERY DECISION IS SEEN AS HELPFUL
FOR ONE REASON OR ANOTHER.**

Personal Insights

What is a meaningful legacy? Money is the obvious answer, but money is often the cause of ugly friction. Friendship can be a legacy, but the hearts involved must keep it alive and that's often a variable. Love can be a legacy, but definitions are individual and not always compatible. I believe that a meaningful legacy is something that doesn't depend on the vagaries of others. As I look back over my life, the only gift that didn't depend on others was the growth I was willing to accept within my heart. It wasn't always easy allowing this growth to manifest, but once I had it, it couldn't be retracted the way money, friendship, or love could be retracted. It was mine because I felt it, regardless of other legacies.

CHAPTER 16

Handicaps

Why do we have handicaps?

**LOVE HAS MANY LOOKS, MANY THOUGHTS,
MANY NAMES, MANY USES,
MANY SYMBOLS, AND MANY ASPIRATIONS.
JUST AS YOU KNOW HOW
TO CHOOSE FOR YOURSELF TODAY,
SO HAVE YOU KNOWN THROUGHOUT MILLENNIA.**

Did you have a handicap, Jesus?

Yes, the obvious one was my temper; the less obvious, my sensitivity.

Why was sensitivity a handicap?

Because it kept me feeling susceptible to the feelings swirling around me, and plenty of times I didn't like what I felt.

Did you dislike those feelings because you had given those feelings to others?

Yes but it took me a while to understand these physics. In the meantime, I cursed what I thought a handicap.

Did you know anyone with a real handicap?

A real handicap was one that pushed a person to find the blessing beyond the pain. In this respect, the soul in its infinite wisdom always chose judiciously.

Did you heal any handicapped people?

I knew handicapped people who were able to heal themselves.

All I did was remind them of the beauty within their hearts.

Was there someone who exemplified this process?

A man by the name of Aaron exemplified this process. Seen by others as odd, that oddity alone was enough to bring him scorn: *You have weird ideas, you talk like an idiot, and you look even stranger.* He went to extremes to handle this feedback, even so far as to scream at his many mockers. But all he ever got was the desperate posturing of others.

Were people cruel to Aaron on purpose?

Yes, but only because they forgot how they would feel on the other end of scorn.

Did it help Aaron to yell at his many mockers?

He thought it would in the moment of his pain, but as he put his energy into vilifying the culprits, he became one. Eventually, he came upon a pamphlet with a message inside that said to look inside his own heart when searching for love.

How naïve, he thought, *I'm happy when people are kind to me and miserable when they aren't.* But the words were well-remembered; it seems that once his soul heard an idea it liked, it worked hard to keep it around.

Was Aaron aware how his negative moods were making his life more difficult?

Yes, but he justified his moods. *Why shouldn't I resent insensitive people, why shouldn't I hate the cruel and unkind, why shouldn't I withdraw from those who treat me badly?* But nothing was quite as devastating as believing that hate was going to heal him only to find it didn't.

When he saw other handicapped people interacting with ease, he resented their ability to do what he could not. Aaron had yet to understand that choosing a mood and choosing a daily wardrobe were exactly the same process.

But clothes were about his personal needs in the moment.

And happiness wasn't? *The act of choosing* was the same regardless of what was being chosen: a wardrobe or a thought.

How could Aaron stay positive when hateful thoughts were attacking?

He couldn't, but he couldn't feel attacked when positive thoughts were held. He rationalized his hate, but hate was hate regardless of why he had it. More importantly, hate lived in illusion. When Aaron invested in *nothing, nothing* is what he got back.

Sooner or later, everyone had reasons to hate. In terms of visual beauty, Aaron did have a handicap. In terms of intellect, he was gifted. In terms of this particular journey, a curious mind and a healthy intellect were a lot more relevant than any look he could have chosen.

Maybe he heard a voice telling him that he was horrible and he couldn't get rid of it.

Maybe he did, but to get rid of it, he had to listen to the voice that said, *You're the glorious love of God.* Opposing views could not be held simultaneously. To him, controlling his mind was a foreign concept, so I asked Aaron to give me his negative thoughts so I could counter productively. Our conversation went like this:

Aaron said: *My thoughts are different from everyone else's.*

That's energy being itself, my friend.

My existence is sad and lonely, he bemoaned.

Your existence is whatever emotion you bring to the process of living.

Raising children has been denied me, he complained.

Raising children is an exercise in growth for those who choose to have them.

My body is useless for athletics, he lamented.

Then your body has a different reason for being.

Others have an easier time than I do, he insisted.

An easy time is the ease you bring to others.

Beauty has a better chance of happiness, he grumbled.

Beauty has the happiness it offers.

Some people don't deserve my love, he asserted.

What if you deserve it anyway?

My childhood taught me that I was not so worthy, he protested.

You've changed your mind about a lot of ideas your childhood taught you, so why can't you reinvestigate this one? Does it feel good to think that you aren't the love of God and everyone else is?

No, he admitted. *More humor would help me.*

You'll find it as soon as you enjoy the person you are today.

Your answers to Aaron were simplistic.

They certainly were. They only got complicated when I told him to change. Then, instead of helping him to appreciate who he was, I made him feel he was wanting. Then both of us were lacking what we needed.

Can you give me more of that conversation you had with him?

Sure. It went like this:

Aaron said: *I'm feeling very unhappy.*

I said: Make others happier so your mood improves immediately.

I want the people around me to embrace my beliefs.

Believe in the right to think uniquely and they will.

I want my friends to be more compassionate

Then be a compassionate friend so compassionate people find you.

I need more attention.

Then give attention to others.

I'm tired of people complaining in the face of my obvious handicaps.

Find the blessings your handicaps have brought you, so those in likeness can find you.

I need more help in reaching my goals.

Then help others to reach theirs.

I want more respect from those who think they are better than I am.

Then respect those you think are less than you are.

I want to get rid of those who drag me down.

Then pull yourself up to the level of admiration you want your mirror to reflect.

I want to get rid of people who forever rehash their lives.

Then go back to yours and find more wonder from living it.

I want to get rid of the people who try to push me around.

Then bless each person in whatever he or she is doing so pushing disappears.

Your philosophy was so inverted.

Only because I spoke of what Aaron must do, not what others must do. But nothing on the outside could fill Aaron's heart completely regardless of where he went or who he happened to find.

Wasn't there a truth that was right for everyone?

Yes, but it was the one that said: each soul had a truth it needed.

If no ultimate truth existed, what was Aaron looking for?

What everyone was looking for: The ultimate in himself.

If everyone's truth was different, what did they have in common?

Their search to find it.

What if Aaron wanted a bigger truth?

A bigger truth was the bigness he saw in others.

What if Aaron wasn't fulfilled at the end of his life?

He lived another lifetime through which to seek fulfillment. His handicap wasn't chosen to block fulfillment; it was chosen to do the opposite and keep him focused on what was real: emotion. Eventually Aaron's handicap forced him to go within. As he realized the depth to which his choices had led him, he could appreciate his creativity instead of pitying his isolation.

Did Aaron live in other lifetimes in which his body was perfect?

Perfect for the trip he had in mind for himself then. Others may not have agreed, but to gain their respect, he had to keep his own belief alive since he always found his mirror.

Was he brave for making his choices?

He was God. This was the body he thought would remind him of that brave fact. Yes, his handicap pushed people away. But, as he pushed through his resistance, others felt his effort to reconnect and pushed through theirs to reciprocate.

Did Aaron seek out beautiful people to compensate him for his ugliness?

Yes, but he always found his mirror: people feeling inadequate trying to find completeness through another. When sadness overwhelmed him, he fell down on his knees in prayer: *Dear God, where is happiness? Where is love? Help me to find it.* A few days later, he heard about a miracle in Jerusalem. In dire need of one himself, he went in search of the healer. I was not the miracle worker Aaron imagined finding. In fact, he postulated to several people around him that my message was simplistic and my presentation juvenile. Nevertheless, he came back to hear me again and again.

Gradually, my positive thoughts permeated his psyche. But as soon as he felt better, ego brought him down again: *Who would believe such drivel, and who are all these idiots here listening to it?*

However, he was one of those idiots listening fairly regularly. It finally dawned on him that whether or not the message was sophisticated, hearing it felt wonderful; whether I had solutions or not, his hadn't worked. What could he lose from trying a few and seeing what happened. When he had a relapse I reassured Aaron that positive action conquered negative thoughts. Still, he battled: *Too easy to work, too good to be true, too late for me.* But eventually, he didn't care how simplistic the message was. He was happy where once he'd been miserable, and that was the answer to his prayer.

What changed for Aaron after he met you?

Where once he'd felt out-of-step, he felt included; where once he'd dreaded the morrow, he valued the moment; where once he'd prayed for companionship, he found a friend in himself; where once he'd looked for love where he couldn't possibly find it, he found it every place he looked. Where once he'd begged for respect, he gave what he had begged for; where once he'd looked for payback for every little gesture, he paid the price of unconditional love; where once he'd questioned my sanity for sticking to my principles, he lived those principles and finally won his sanity. He thought his friendship with me was a miracle because what had seemed impossible became possible.

I thought miracles were the revelation of God in some incredible way.

That's what Aaron thought had happened. God had revealed the beauty in him and he felt incredible having it.

I mean in terms of spirit materializing right in front of him.

Spirit materialized before him rather frequently. Spirit didn't withhold itself from Aaron; spirit was seen in whatever way his heart was open to feeling it. In fact, how could it be otherwise? He knew the souls he wanted to welcome into his life.

Were those get-togethers two-way decisions?

All get-togethers were two way decisions. Souls bonded when unions were timely, regardless of where they bonded or who those bonds included.

Were those who bonded in a war on a loving path, too?

War was simply a word that described a certain kind of union. Like-minded souls were still progressing, just in a bond that said *I need to fight to get what I want.* Some of our so-called peaceful movements had more warring in them than some of our so-called warring ones did, but the living of one's mirror was always the same. War didn't come to Aaron in any conventional sense, but he still learned that hell-bent actions created the hell envisioned.

How could Aaron's answers be emotional if his handicap was physical?

How could strength come to Aaron through negativity if power was the love of God? To gain more faith in the rightness of life, he had to enjoy the rightness of every day.

Did you give Aaron a prayer to help him as he progressed?

Yes, it went like this.

Dear God:

My love remains my knowledge forever.

My heart remains my friend forever.

My aura remains my self forever.

Help me to share the person I am, so all that I am expands forever.

THE BODY HAS TWO REASONS FOR BEING.
ONE, TO ADORE YOU.
AND TWO, TO BE ADORED.

Worksheet Section:

Chapter 16 – Handicaps

What do you consider your biggest handicap?

How has this handicap forced you to know more depth?

How has this depth broadened your outlook?

With whom can you share your depth in order to ease their pain?

Who shared their depth with you, and how did it help?

Questions to Ponder:

- *Do I speak to impress others or to express the love in my heart?*
- *Do I wait for others to make me happy or do I try to make others happy?*
- *Do I expect people to love me or do I share the love that I feel?*

GRACIOUS BEHAVIOR IS GIVEN TO OTHERS FOR THE SAKE OF YOUR OWN EVOLVUTIONARY PROCESS.

Personal Insights

I don't have a handicap that catches the eye of another; nonetheless, I have one. I believe everyone does to one degree or another. Some handicaps are obvious; some hidden; some short-lived; some long-term. But regardless of when or how they manifest, they offer the growth needed. Perhaps the handicap is less important than how it is handled, for how it is handled is the handling that returns. I have a choice: I can use my handicap to accelerate love and compassion, or, I can use my handicap to stunt interaction; thereby becoming a truly handicapped person.

CHAPTER 17

Betrayal

Why is betrayal so painful?

BETRAYAL IS AN ACT OF DOING IN A WAY YOU'D HATE TO BE DONE TO.

Wasn't betrayal an issue for some of your friends, Jesus?

It was.

Did they mirror some betrayal in you?

Had I felt betrayed they would have. But mirrors were emotional, not pictorial. At the end of my journey, I understood their growth and praised their participation. Therefore, respect was my emotion, not the feeling of betrayal.

Judas betrayed you, didn't he?

Judas betrayed himself, as outward actions reflected inward actions.

Did betrayal return to him regardless of how he betrayed?

Betrayal returned to him regardless of whom he betrayed. If Judas betrayed others, he was betrayed by others. If he betrayed himself, betrayal poisoned the mind. Once in the mind it moved to the body. But regardless of how betrayal returned, it told him what he needed to know of self.

Did his body actually betray him?

No, he in fact betrayed his body. And he betrayed it the same way he betrayed a friend: by undermining that union. Undermining a union meant that he took an action with someone else that he didn't want taken with him.

If Judas repeated a rumor, did he create betrayal?

He created whatever emotion went along with the rumor.

How could he stop betraying?

By making himself the subject of the rumor and acting accordingly. More importantly rumors lived in illusion and were misleading. Therefore, as Judas misconstrued the rumors he repeated, he was misconstrued by the rumors said about him.

Can you give me an example of a rumor misconstrued?

Sure. When I returned from solitude, someone told Judas that I was seeing God within each person. Judas spread that rumor, but changed the meaning behind the words by saying that I had a power no one else had. As he insinuated skills in me that others were somehow lacking, he attracted those insinuating a lack of potential in him. But the words he spoke did not create his mirror; the emotion behind them did.

When Judas betrayed you, did he humiliate his family and disgust his friends?

No, he attracted betrayal back. Humiliation and disgust were only felt when given.

How could betrayal come back to him when he died right after betraying?

The fact that he dropped his body didn't stop the force of physics. He lived what he had given in one way or another.

Judas only betrayed me from a belief that something good would result; and the good he sought was the continued presence of me right here on Earth.

Why would Judas think you'd still be around if he turned you in to be crucified?

He didn't turn me in to be crucified; he turned me in, in hopes of seeing me get out of town quickly. He assumed that I would do what he would have done had the soldiers been after him. I had no intention of leaving and refused to take the bait.

Had Judas been honest with himself, he would have admitted that he was acting on his own behalf, not mine. But all he could hear was the voice of doom telling him over and over, *How will you find your spiritual growth if your spiritual leader is dead?*

Unwilling to question his delusional theory that I was responsible for his expanded growth, he attacked what he thought delusional in me. *Why are you still here,* he asked, *when I've told you the soldiers are coming?*

Rather than explain my motives, I tried to get Judas to look at his. *Why do you feel such angst, my friend? Is it my refusal to get out of town or your refusal to get out of town? And who is not being mindful of his needs, you or me?*

Judas understood. His instincts had been urging him to get out of town for weeks. But how could he trust those instincts while doubting mine? Doubt was doubt regardless of why he had it.

Wouldn't leaving have been running away from his problems?

Yes, but running away would have been helpful had it given him time to reassess. The irony was that I wouldn't have been the friend he wanted had I listened to him instead of myself.

Didn't Judas turn you in to save his skin?

Yes, but to Judas, saving his skin meant keeping me alive, and well within his reach. Therefore, he did whatever he thought would make that happen. In terms of the illusion he was right.

To me, saving my skin meant remembering my reality, or the love within my heart. Therefore, I kept my focus where the payoff was for me.

When I was arrested, Judas was distraught. Convinced that meaningful progress was over in terms of his life, he did himself in. But death was no more traumatic than waking up from a bad dream. He realized instantly how wise I had been to trust myself.

Wouldn't his loved ones have forgiven him his betrayal?

Their forgiveness was not the problem; forgiving himself was.

But Judas was only trying to help you, wasn't he?

He was only trying to help himself, but even this tender thought eluded him. All he could hear was the voice of ego screaming in his ear, *What will everyone think of you? What will everyone believe of you? How will everyone judge you?*

Did Judas kill himself rather then face his family?

He thought so, but facing himself was the problem.

How did you view his act of suicide, Jesus?

The same way I viewed every decision he made: for the help it offered his soul. By the time he committed suicide I knew that resurrection was eternal, even if suicide was the way he chose to live it.

How could suicide be a resurrection?

How could it not be if resurrection represented the rebirthing of energy? It wasn't the optimal choice of renewal, since Judas was already living the optimal choice, but every decision brought him growth eventually.

Didn't Judas betray you for the bribe that he received?

Judas took the money, but he saw the bribe as a way of forcing a certain picture; a picture he thought would get him what he needed. He didn't succeed, of course, because if Judas wanted to get what he needed, he had to confront his own controlling nature, and look within for answers instead of making me the only person who had them.

Maybe he didn't have faith in his ability to do that.

Maybe he didn't, but to gain faith, he had to at least make the effort. How else could he attract people who were willing to make an effort on his behalf?

Did Judas feel worthy of being helped?

Not then. But to feel worthier, he only had to help others feel worthy.

What if he had hateful feelings?

He needed to express them. Judas only hated because he believed that others were preventing him from getting what he wanted.

Did Judas feel that life was unfair?

Yes, but to feel that life was fair, he had to see everyone as equally advantaged.

But they weren't.

You must be referring to the picture again. In the reality of emotion, everyone had the same fair chance to succeed.

What would have changed had Judas believed in fairness?

If the thought of unfairness was making him miserable, he would have felt better.

Did he have any other issues besides the one of betrayal?

In the big picture of evolution, he had many, not always with a brain through which to think but always with a heart through which to feel.

What good was an experience if Judas couldn't think while in it?

What good was a brain if he couldn't love while using it?

Did you want Judas to follow your lead?

I wanted everyone to follow my lead from the time I was old enough to reason. When I knew the ultimate prize was a feeling to be experienced, not a place to be led to, I urged people to listen to themselves.

Would Judas have been happier had different people been with him?

He would have been happier had he welcomed the people who were. To improve his future, he had to focus on the feelings he wanted instead of the people he thought should be there. Even after he dropped his body, he had to welcome whoever showed up.

Did he have many friends?

He had quite a few. Judas was well liked by the people around him. Had he not been such a bright and sensitive individual, he wouldn't have been so devastated by his own inner frailties. He judged others harshly because he judged himself harshly. Then, he interpreted the inner workings of them according to the inner workings of him.

When his healing skills improved in other lifetimes, was there more and more to heal?

As his healing skills improved, there was less and less to heal, not more and more.

How do you think of Judas now, Jesus?

I think of him as a teacher, and a great one at that. Judas was the living proof that action/reaction worked. The words, do unto others as you would have them do unto you, were well remembered as Judas lived the opposite.

What was one of Judas' greatest weaknesses?

His inability to stand against the majority; he always wanted to be on the winning side. Therefore, regardless of how many times the power shifted, he shifted with it.

When he saw me getting popular, he was right there beside me basking in all that glory. When he saw me getting into trouble for being popular, he disengaged. Judas didn't wish me any suffering; he just didn't want to suffer because of me.

Did anything beneficial happen because of that betrayal?

I thought so. I sensed that many would falter in their paths toward oneness and I hoped that all who witnessed Judas' choice, and the torture that followed, would use that torment to inspire greater efforts on their own behalf.

THERE IS ONLY ONE OF US HERE.
WHATEVER YOU GIVE,
YOU GIVE TO YOURSELF.
IF LOVE IS ABSENT,
YOU'RE IN BETRAYAL

Worksheet Section:

Chapter 17 – Betrayal

Have you betrayed yourself?

Have you betrayed others?

How have you been betrayed?

How have you handled betrayal?

Has your handling ended betrayal or perpetrated it?

Questions to Ponder:

- *Do I wonder if life will reward me, or do I praise the reward I have?*
- *Do I honor each person's uniqueness, or do I look for ways to separate?*
- *Do I love my lessons and share my growth, or do I loathe my lessons and hate my growth?*

YOU ARE MERCIFUL AND YOU ARE GOOD WHEN YOU ARE AWARE OF PHYSICS.

Personal Insights

I deplore the thought of betrayal. But like it or not, it's with me in little ways I often fail to notice: a remark about a friend, a whispered rumor, an exaggerated fact. Because I think of betrayal as a sin of huge proportions, I delude myself when the small ones make an appearance. But action/reaction has no investment in size; it reads my every offering and reciprocates. When the boomerang returns in all its accelerated thrust, my first reaction is outrage; my second is help! Jesus is always there to guide me:

Would you want what you did, done to you? That's all you need to ask. If you wouldn't, don't do it. Like it or not, it will return and slap you in the face with the added power of physics.

CHAPTER 18

Identities

What is our real identity?

NAMES, TITLES, AND PLACES LOSE THEIR VALIDITY AS SOON AS YOU LEAVE THE HUMAN PLANE. THE EMOTION BEHIND THEM LASTS FOREVER.

Names, titles, and places were a part of your experience, though, weren't they, Jesus?

Part of my illusionary experience, yes, but they didn't reveal my inner journey, or the search for my reality.

Don't we know more about your inner journey through the many stories told?

We know more about the inner journeys of the many different story-tellers, since each had a history of individual clarity.

Can those stories be trusted?

Why must they be? Only the love in those stories makes them relevant to you.

Was there an incident that was especially important to you?

There was one that involved a soldier by the name of Vrotskuv, who entered my life to confirm my faith in goodness.

Did Vrotskuv have any faith in you?

He gained more faith as he sensed my faith in him; he was the soldier responsible for delivering prisoners to the sites of their crucifixions. When the people lined the streets that day in loving support of me, they took up a chant to let me know of their presence. Vrotskuv got uneasy. Rightly or wrongly he saw them a threat. One voice inside his head urged him to hurt the heretic if he wanted to feel in charge. The other voice urged him to feel in charge by honoring the heretic.

Brushing the latter voice aside, he looked for an easy insult to show the crowd that he was the one in charge here. His opportunity came when I stopped to assist a fellow prisoner struggling under the weight of his heavy cross.

In the process of helping him to regain his balance, the robe padding my shoulder fell to the ground. Vrotskuv picked it up and stood there, daring me to defy him. Instead of seeing the anger he expected, he saw only love.

Startled, he couldn't believe the message he was receiving: *We are all in charge of ourselves in the love of God forever.* Intellectually, it didn't compute; emotionally, it impacted deeply, so deeply that Vrotskuv was determined to feel it again.

Because he wanted to cherish himself or because he wanted to cherish you?

Somehow they seemed like one and the same. Instead of seeing the thief who lived in Vrotskuv, I saw the God who lived in Vrotskuv and, then, he saw it too. That moment was so powerfully felt that it took a burst of chanting to get him back to the task. For the rest of the day, he thought about that encounter. What had he seen in my eyes that had stirred his emotions so deeply? Irritated that he couldn't explain it, he grabbed the robe and set out to give it back, hoping a second encounter would clarify the previous one.

As he laid the robe at the foot of the cross and looked in my eyes again, the feeling returned. It deepened into a vision, revealing to him all that he had lived and all that he could live; an all-inclusive moment, neither human nor ethereal, but a feeling merging the two. Factored in time it equaled seconds; factored in emotion, eons.

It came to him, not as a payback for the past but as a blueprint for the future, whether that future was here or elsewhere, now or later, conscious or unconscious. After the vision ended, no words were shared but the message was clear: *Welcome home*. From that moment forth, everything Vrotskuv did was to keep that moment alive in whatever else he was doing.

In the weeks that followed, he located many of my friends, hoping that one of them would see him as I had. None did, but inadvertently he discovered why. I had accepted him unconditionally, knowing full well who he was and the job he was there to do. My friends accepted him grudgingly; fearful of what would happen to them if they didn't. But even in the presence of fear and animosity, Vrotskuv courted their acquaintance, willing to endure any rudeness in order to find some answers.

Many introductions later, Vrotskuv convinced Peter to invite him to one of his meetings. It didn't take long for Vrotskuv to notice a theme that kept recurring: *We always find ourselves in the people we face*. Pondering what that meant in terms of his interaction with me, he concluded that his heart had merged with mine, and to live that merger again, he had to live that merger with others. He found that union by asking how he'd feel if, every time he looked into the eyes of another, he felt my heart again. Naturally, as he told himself that I was in the every heart he faced, he couldn't wait to find me there.

Did Vrotskuv feel terrible after stealing the robe?

He felt terrible when his mirror showed up to remind him of his behavior. He only stopped stealing when he knew himself as the person stolen from.

Would he have stopped stealing had he thought his behavior known?

Had he understood that others reacted accordingly, yes.

Vrotskuv wanted honest people in his life. In the end, high-minded motives didn't change his life; his desire to receive the honorable in others did. To stay mindful of his goal, he said to himself as he gave to others, *Here is a gift to myself.*

When his mirror was insecure, was Vrotskuv insecure?

Until he was honest about it; then honesty replaced insecurity.

Even if that honesty was horrible?

Honesty wasn't horrible or wonderful; honesty simply was.

What did Vrotskuv learn about prosperity in this lifetime?

He learned that prosperity had more to do with abundance within than abundance without. But if Vrotskuv needed funds for his evolution, funds were made available.

Did he do something wrong if funds were not available?

Not if the right in his life was honored.

Did money come when Vrotskuv did what he loved?

Fulfillment came when he did what he loved. Fulfillment didn't have any requisite look, only a requisite feeling.

What incentives did Vrotskuv need in order to live more wisely?

Incentives varied. They were anything from a new friend, to a new day, to a new lifetime, depending on what was needed.

Did Peter's friends welcome Vrotskuv at the meeting he attended?

Some did; quite a few were resentful. Vrotskuv was a soldier as well as a stranger with nothing to recommend him but his need to find some answers. His constant talk of his vision annoyed quite a few, some even questioned whether he'd had one. And those who did believe were envious. *Why did this happen to him and not to us? He's a nobody, while we've been following Jesus for years.*

Vrotskuv discovered that those who had known me on a daily basis were every bit as individually disposed as those who hadn't. In fact, several who'd known me as a friend were worried about their complicity in my fate. To appease their guilty consciences, they decided that any action they had or hadn't taken was excusable since I had help in ways that they did not.

As they believed in special help, they created separation instead of oneness, and oneness with the whole was how I found my help. Unwilling to accept responsibility for their own victim mentality, they looked for someone to blame; Vrotskuv was handy. But even facing their angry accusations, Vrotskuv didn't back down; he was more concerned with personal growth than impersonal resentment.

Did their feelings of victimization have any other drawback?

Yes, it caused them to forget the properties of spontaneous resurrection: self-responsibility, self-determination and self-enlightenment. As loss overwhelmed them and depression set in, they insisted that I would still be alive if people like Vrotskuv weren't.

Even though I resurrected to prove that I was alive, ego rebutted here as well: *Only someone who rose from the dead can be the love of God.* And holding this one definition to explain divinity, they lost all faith in themselves. Then, to feel better, they looked for agreement.

What about those who didn't lose faith?

They were busy enacting their own resurrections.

Did anyone challenge Vrotskuv in terms of his vision?

Yes, but for him, the vision had been emotional; he didn't see how anyone could successfully challenge that.

What did he learn from the few who were kind to him?

More about himself.

Did Vrotskuv think of you as wise?

Wise for my journey, yes, but he suspected that everyone was the wisdom of God personified in form.

How could all those people have been God?

Who else would God have been?

A divine energy that was met upon their death.

Why would God be revealed to them out-of-form but not in-form? Seeking answers where none existed was the ultimate frustration.

What about the God who greeted them when they died?

God greeted them most assuredly, but as soon as they were met, they knew they'd been this greeter many times themselves. Just as they loved and supported their friends in-matter, they loved and supported them out-of-matter. Some didn't believe in the notion of God, but everyone knew the feeling of love; and everyone could expand it.

Did Vrotskuv see himself as a sensitive person?

He saw himself as an honest person. If he was cruel, he took responsibility for his cruelty. In his opinion, many followers did not. They rationalized their cruelty, calling it *absolute truth.* To Vrotskuv, their absolute truth was cruel because it said to others: *We have the answer to heaven on Earth and anyone not believing in us will never find it.* But anyone who claimed to have the one true answer to heaven on Earth had effectively shut the door to heaven. Heaven was felt through an open, accepting heart.

Did Vrotskuv respect many of your followers?

Yes, and if they knew something he didn't, he wanted to know them better. He sensed that several hoped to establish more authority by insisting that true believers preached what they preached: that I was the Son of God and no one else was. Vrotskuv honored what he believed instead.

He knew that I had referred to myself as God, but he also knew that I had referred to my friends as God, and my enemies, too. Few were repeating that line. Government retaliation was still an active force. But even after it wasn't, many followers didn't want the masses seeing themselves as the same authority they were. Then they had a dilemma. How could they have faith in themselves while telling others that faith in oneself was unwise?

Vrotskuv decided to investigate within, sure in the knowledge that progress would always be obvious by the progress of those around him.

GOD IS THE LOVE WITHIN.
REALITY IS THE LOVE YOU LIVE.
YOU ARE THE EVERYTHING THESE TWO INCLUDE.

Worksheet Section:

Chapter 18 – Identities

In your opinion, what qualities must a person have to live as God in humanness?

Where are some of those qualities being lived?

When those qualities are present, isn't that person God-like?

When those qualities are absent, has this person suddenly ceased to exist?

Haven't you learned more about who you want to be from who you don't want to be?

Questions to Ponder:

- *Who inspires me more: a perfect person, or a person overcoming obstacles?*
- *Who supports me more: a static person, or a person sensing potential?*
- *Who do I want to be more: a person smugly satisfied, or a person looking for growth?*

THE GREATEST ACHIEVEMENT
YOU'LL EVER REACH
IS TO LOVE AND ACCEPT YOURSELF.

Personal Insights

I believe that God is a power within–not a power that is only met upon death. If that's true, it simplifies things, don't you think? No more dialogues about whose God is valid and whose God is not since every soul is equally valid. No more wars in the name of God since God is you, me, and everyone. No more posturing that God told me to do this and God told me to say that since God isn't separate from the speaker. No more worries about taking the name of God in vain since you might as well be cursing yourself. No more religions claiming that they have the one true path, since every path that offers a person love is the path of true redemption. No more guilt for breaking God's rules since the rules we have are the ones we've given ourselves.

CHAPTER 19

Hatred

What does hate create?

**QUEST AS A BELIEVER
INSTEAD OF A NON-BELIEVER.
ENERGY ATTEMPTS TO PROVE
WHATEVER IT THEORIZES AS SO.**

Did you know many people whose hearts were full of hate, Jesus?

Yes, and I knew myself as one of them. When I hated, it was always for the same reason: people were denying me what I needed and I held them responsible for my loss.

Who around you had a similar struggle?

Everyone had a similar struggle at one time or another; especially my friend, Mary.

The Mary who was a prostitute?

The Mary who came to think of herself as one. I saw her as a friend, someone I admired for making brave choices. I also saw her as the sister of Lazarus, a man I cared for deeply.

Were Mary and Lazarus emotionally close to each other?

As toddlers they were close. Later, Mary couldn't befriend anyone without her father's wrath. If Lazarus tried to befriend her anyway, he was beaten for his efforts. He suspected the truth about his father and his relationship with Mary, especially after hearing the whispers of his father's friends, but Mary never spoke of her father's abuse. He promised death to her if she did, and to anyone she told. She believed her father since he was the all-powerful force in her household, and anything he ordered to happen, happened.

When did Mary know he was bluffing?

She never knew he was bluffing. He could have killed her many times over. Mary believed she was born to serve her father; and no one had told her differently. But it still didn't make any sense to her. Why was she singled out for such mental, physical and emotional abuse? She wanted her life to be different, but first she had to see herself differently.

How could Mary build on abuse in a positive way?

By loving herself in spite of the abuser.

If Mary was autonomous to choose any path she wanted, why did she choose this one?

To prove to herself that even this choice could lead a person to love. When she planned her journey, it seemed like the only path that made any sense.

Was it fair for her to endure this trauma?

Fair in the picture, no; fair in the heart, yes.

Wasn't there someone Mary could go to for help?

She didn't think so. Abuse was rampant in her society, for the rich and poor alike. In fact, Mary came from relative means, but money didn't protect her from an abusive father. Even the rabbi avoided dealing with incest if powerful patrons were involved, and the officials had little sympathy for those they often patronized. The hunters were left to govern themselves and the prey were left to fend for themselves.

Mary lost her virginity at seven. After her father tired of her, he shared her with his friends; they took their cue from him:

You're a slut, you're a pig, and you're a no-account whore. You deserve to suffer, you deserve to die, so get on with it.

Was anyone kind to Mary?

I was kind to Mary by expecting the same accountability from her that I expected from everyone else. She didn't always think I was being kind but, eventually, she felt the impact of equal treatment, and reassessed all that she thought she'd come here to live. Her life was strewn with setbacks, but eventually she was able to see her father as the man who had pushed her to save herself instead of the villain who had ruined her life.

Wasn't it only natural for her to hate her father?

It was predictable; she understood hate. And giving up what she understood for something she didn't, seemed pretty risky to her. She had survived, however. At least she could appreciate that.

To handle her hate, she had to put herself at the helm of her experience instead of at the effect. True, she couldn't control her father, but she could control her response to his behavior.

Did Mary feel important because of her friendship with you?

I wasn't considered an important person to know. In our community, Mary was considered more important than I was. She valued our friendship because I helped her to sense a courage she hadn't known existed. When she asked me how I defined courage, I said it was the willingness to love even in the face of reasons not to.

Did Mary lash out at her father?

As she grew older she did. After one particularly ugly confrontation, she came to me with so many injuries she could hardly walk. I suggested that lashing out was not the panacea she hoped for, and perhaps she was making her life more difficult.

Mary was aghast. *How can that be? If I don't lash out, the pain will only go deeper.*

Which do you prefer, I said, *the pain from lashing out over and over or the pain from abstinence once? At least with the latter the pain is temporary. With the former, the pain repeats itself again and again until you're either too sick to respond or too dead to care.*

Mary didn't want to be even more traumatized than she already was. *How can I release an abuser who treats me like scum? What will change? Would I be safe? Will I be happy? More importantly, why am I the one to change? I'm the victim, aren't I?*

I reminded her that victimization was more about attitude than circumstances.

She was shocked by that possibility, but shock didn't prevent her from hoping I was right. Filled with doubt but willing to prove it bogus, she decided that she could at least be more pleasant around her father even if that was all she could manage.

Just as Mary had feared would happen, he was meaner than ever. When she came to me and complained, I told her to release her conditions on who was supposed to respond. Then, maybe she'd notice how big her heart was getting.

Was Mary able to manage her anger constructively?

To manage her anger constructively was to get her anger out. Cursing helped her to do that. But words were only noises, and noises lived in illusion. The emotion behind them was her reality. In the final analysis, cursing helped Mary to express her feelings, so cursing was the solution in terms of managing her anger.

What prepared Mary for living in happier times?

Living in hell.

What happened to people who had big challenges and still couldn't find their way?

They received help, too, from those in similar dilemmas.

Mary had to move out of the conceptual and into the literal, i.e. each person was her. As she brought this theory to life, she didn't want to hurt herself.

Why was her father abusive?

Because he couldn't find a better way to relate to the people around him. He felt no joy in life; therefore, he didn't want anyone else to either.

If Mary had moments of happiness she hid them, knowing that if her father sensed them, he would level the field with cruelty. He got that cruelty back, of course, even from Mary, as she avenged on him in passive aggressive ways, causing him untold sorrows, and leaving him feeling used and abused as well.

Her favorite method of torture was to talk about him behind his back with every man who used her. These men, doubting her father's loyalty, and thinking they had to undermine him to save themselves, betrayed him at every turn.

Did her father try to doubt Mary into submission?

He didn't have to; she submitted rather than die. But try as he might, he couldn't access Mary's inner world; the part of her that mystified him. Whatever mystified him he feared; whatever he feared he abused.

Did Mary think of respect as her ideal?

Yes, but ideals had to valued; to be valued they had to be lived. When Mary dropped her body she didn't take her ideals with her; she took the love she found from having them.

Did the apostles criticize you for befriending Mary?

They criticized my naiveté; sure that Mary would use me badly. When that didn't happen, they said she would hurt my platform. When that didn't happen, they shunned her. When that didn't work, they adjusted, not always graciously, but they adjusted.

What contribution did Mary bring to your ministry?

Her own ministry, as she willingly shared her wisdom with those in similar straits.

Did Mary have times when she wanted to die?

She had times of thinking she'd be better off dead, but she wanted to be better off alive; she just couldn't figure out why it should be so. Waiting for others to give her a reason added to her confusion, since people only came here with their own reasons for being.

She confessed to me that she didn't love her father. I told her she didn't have to love him; she only had to release him. To release him she had to remember that, if she was only searching for love in the midst of her personal turmoil, he was only searching for love in the midst of his.

Didn't you give Mary a reason to live?

I showed her my reason and that was helpful. She watched me treat others as I hoped to be treated; then she treated her father as she hoped to be treated. She watched me release others in order to feel released; then she released her father from blame so she could release herself from blame. She watched me give the acceptance I wanted back. Then she accepted her father's behavior as the best he could do so she could accept her behavior as the best she could do. She watched me give the love I hoped to receive; then she released her father to his search for love so she could better understand hers.

Was that really enough to rid her of hate?

It was pretty hard to hate a man she knew was searching for love.

How could she be sure of his motivation?

Because she was sure of hers.

What happened to her father after he died?

He went on living.

Did he face God?

Yes, he faced God, but the God he faced was a God who had lived as he had. Once her father dropped his body, the world of emotion was his only reality. Then he realized that his fears and anxieties were the love he had closed his heart to. But he couldn't ignore the judgment in his soul since his soul was all that he had.

What about the consequences of his behavior?

The consequences came as he lived what he had given.

Could Mary heal with her father out-of-body, even if she was in-body?

Sure. She only had to share her truth and release him to his.

That didn't guarantee repentance.

No, but Mary's healing was not dependent on his repentance; it was dependent on her ability to forgive herself and move on.

Don't you mean to forgive her father?

No, I mean that she had to forgive herself before she could change her life.

Did Mary ever find total devotion?

She always found the love she had given to others. As her knowledge deepened, her partners' matched it.

Would her life have been more difficult had she not been a friend of yours?

Our desire to be together was created in reality, and nothing in illusion could change that.

Did Mary find a reward from being here this lifetime?

Yes, but her biggest reward came from her biggest challenge.

Why?

Because the contrast between forgiveness and hatred was so illuminating.

**FIGHTING THE WOES OF THE WORLD
IS A BOTTOMLESS PIT.
YOU ONLY KNOW
HOW TO END YOUR OWN
AND SET A HEALTHY EXAMPLE.**

Worksheet Section:

Chapter 19 – Hatred

Who in your life is the least deserving of love?

If you knew this person was suffering deeply, could you be more compassionate?

If you knew this soul had a deep respect for you, could you be more tolerant?

If you knew this person would eventually beg you for your forgiveness, could you be more merciful?

If you knew this person's path had once been yours, could you forgive yourself?

Questions to Ponder:

- *Which has greater impact–dreaming up a fantasy or watching it unfold?*
- *Which encourages growth more–following the crowd or taking lovely detours?*
- *Which stays with you longer–learning to create or loving your creations?*

NO ONE USES YOU IN YOUR LIFETIME
YOU USE YOUR LIFETIME TO ENLIGHTEN SELF.

Personal Insights

If Jesus is right, and we don't take our ideals with us when we leave here–only the love we found from having them–it simplifies things, don't you think? No one is proven to have had the wrong or the right beliefs; only to have loved the ones embraced. No one is proven to have lived in the wrong or the right religion; only to have admired the ones lived. No one is proven to have favored the wrong or the right path; only to have made the most of the ones chosen. No one is proven to have honored the wrong or the right talent; only to have honored the ones revealed. No one is proven to have asked the wrong or the right questions; only to have thrived on the answers found. No one is proven to have loved the wrong or the right God; only to have loved the God it was.

CHAPTER 20

Memories

Are memories controllable?

**TO REMEMBER YOUR PAST IS ONE THING.
TO REMEMBER IT CLEARLY IS ANOTHER.**

What did it mean for you to remember the past clearly, Jesus?

It meant for me to remember the growth it brought to the present.

Even if that memory was awful?

Yes, since a memory was only awful if the good it wrought was ignored.

Who also struggled to remember the past through growth?

Kiev struggled to remember the past through growth. He and I encountered one another for a few moments in time, but his memory of our union was more powerfully felt than most visual memories he had.

In early childhood, he fell down a flight of steps and went into a coma. His father, Guido, upset by the doctors' prognoses, made a radical decision. The radical he sought was me; not because he believed I could heal Kiev, but because his wife needed some closure.

As I cradled Kiev in my arms, the beauty of oneness transformed the child's being. In fact, that bonding was so intense that Kiev spent the rest of his life trying to relive it.

Was it hard for Guido to accept the help of a stranger?

It was hard for Guido to accept the help of anyone; especially a roaming Haggai of dubious reputation. However, he wasn't about to let his personal qualms interfere with a healing.

When Kiev recovered, Guido was ecstatic. I reassured him that I hadn't healed Kiev any more than I had made him sick in the first place; I had only demonstrated the healthy heart of God and invited Kiev to participate.

Guido was grateful his son had healed and didn't care what explanation I offered; he only cared that his son was well. To show his gratitude, he deeded one of his homes to me, which I in turn used to encourage more healings.

Kiev stayed healthy, and Guido was torn between his need to honor me, and his need to honor his up and coming career; his career won out. His wife, Judith, chose independently and continued her friendship with me.

Guido's career accelerated to the point where he decided that a man in his position couldn't have a wife associated with a controversial figure like me. Judith resisted Guido's wishes but eventually capitulated. Although she revered my teachings, she revered her role in society even more. Judith forgot that our friendship was a heart connection not a picture connection, and she didn't think she could have both: the life she loved and the presence she loved. But instead of taking responsibility for cutting me out of her life, she blamed her husband for all her pain and sorrow.

Did Kiev hear about you while he was growing up?

Yes, although he rarely heard me mentioned inside his household. Guido felt guilty for abandoning me to my fate, and Judith felt angry for succumbing to her husband's dictates. On the other hand, both cared about preserving their relationship with each other.

Later in life, Kiev insisted on hearing the details of his

healing, so they at least indulged him this way.

How did Kiev deal with his unhappy memories?

How they impacted depended on how he held them: either in painful anger or grateful growth. As a child he suppressed them. As an adult, he acknowledged them, analyzed them, and gave thanks for their inspiration.

What bad memories did he have?

Most involved a father who misunderstood him and, therefore, tried to turn him into someone he could understand. Ironically, he and his father were very much alike, both pursuing their goals with equal enthusiasm.

Guido believed that the picture revealed their likeness, and since he favored the one he had, that of a highly placed official, he pushed his son to follow in his footsteps. Kiev wanted to teach. Guido didn't object to the academia, only to the direction in which Kiev wanted to take it: reform.

Embarrassed by Kiev's politics, Guido blamed his anxieties on his son's activities instead of his activities. Then he wanted Kiev to change. But the more he pushed for change, the more Kiev persevered.

Given some of the pickles Kiev got himself into, the government tolerated him with remarkable patience. Kiev was grateful for that protection. But the very reason his safety was insured and that of others was not was the very reason he sought reform.

As he matured and became more curious about his healing, he sought out those who had known me. As he learned about my teachings, he wanted to share them. To share them he had to understand them. To understand them he had to live them. To live them he had to honor his priorities, not his father's priorities. Had he sacrificed his happiness to indulge Guido's, the reason for their union would have been missed. And the reason for their union was the love and release they could offer to one another.

Did Kiev openly oppose his father?

He ridiculed his father's philosophy as harshly as Guido ridiculed his. Kiev thought it was fine to challenge Guido's interests, but not fine for Guido to challenge his. Kiev thought his goals were holier; ergo the same rules did not apply. Sure of his logic, Kiev continued to buck the system, causing trouble with the very people Guido considered his friends.

The conflict accelerated and Guido reassessed. *Why should I continue getting my son out of scrapes when I don't agree with what he's doing to get himself into them in the first place?* Kiev didn't like his father's reversal but he understood it. And rather than cause more friction, he left Jerusalem with every intention of sharing his new beliefs.

Did he leave from a fear of what would happen if he stayed?

Yes but the nature of his fear was emotional, not physical.

Isn't it possible to live around upheaval and still find inner peace?

It's possible. And theoretically, Kiev could have stayed in Jerusalem and gotten out of blame, but if growth was better served by leaving, then not leaving would have repressed that growth. While it's true that Kiev's happiness was not dependent on the picture he saw with his eyes, he often needed a new picture to prove that point to himself.

When Kiev traveled, did he feel your spirit with him, Jesus?

Very much so; he trusted the resurrection and believed that I was just as much with him in the present, as I had been in the past. He was sure that spirit is, regardless of where it is.

Did Kiev believe you were special?

For a while he did. The irony was that his healing would not have occurred had he believed in *specialness*; separation would have occurred instead of the miracle of oneness. He healed because he hadn't yet been told that he was less, or more, than the man who stood before him, cradling him in his arms.

Was Kiev able to remember this beautiful concept as he matured?

Not always, he struggled to remember that beautiful ideas had a life of their own. They didn't need to be pushed on others; example was the tool for teaching.

In what way was Kiev similar to you?

Both of us were sensitive men indifferent to worldly achievement; both of us were bachelors; both of us loved traveling; and both of us were attracted to teaching.

Guido saw his son as so impressed with his healing that he was making a career out of it. As far as Kiev was concerned, the more he resembled me, the more he believed in his path. However, comparisons were not made in his youth. Kiev was a meek and mild child. Not because he was a weakling, but because he was strong enough to honor his needs instead of the needs of his father.

If "meek and mild" described Kiev's youth, why wasn't he compared to your meek and mild childhood?

Because I didn't have one; I was obstreperous, getting into mischief on a fairly regular basis.

How could you be sensitive and obstreperous at the same time?

Easily. Sensitivity referred to within, obstreperous to without.

How else did Guido push Kiev?

He tried to push him into marriage. Kiev considered a bride, but he and Ruth couldn't agree on how to live their lives. Ruth found it inconceivable that Kiev might prefer the life of a roving missionary to that of being her husband.

In Ruth's opinion, he should take his rightful place in Jerusalem society with her beside him, of course. With a chasm like this, they had no common ground upon which to build a future. Yes, they loved each other and, yes, they preferred a love-match to an arranged one. Beyond that, they couldn't agree on anything. Kiev suffered his *poor me* attitude until he realized that he was every bit as responsible for the falling out as she was.

He tried to stay in touch with Ruth but she was not receptive. To her, Kiev was the reason she eventually married a man she grew to dislike. And so great was her blame, she hated the very thought of Kiev. Ruth misconstrued the source of all her misery. It wasn't because she lost the love of Kiev; it was because she didn't appreciate the love she already had.

Kiev struggled too. *Now you've done it,* ego screamed in his ear. *You've lost the one person who could make you happy. Feel sorry for yourself if you want to feel any better.* Then he felt worse. *Now you've done it,* encouraged guilt, and guilt felt awful. *You've lost the one person who can make you happy* made him forget the one person who could: himself. *Feel sorry for yourself if you want to feel any better,* told him to stay depressed if he wanted to heal: an impossible equation. He recovered, but only after he stopped bemoaning his losses and started living his dreams.

How could he expect Ruth to leave all that was familiar to go off somewhere with him?

He didn't expect her to; his expectations were the problem. Should he succumb to his love for her and give up his dream of travel, or should he pursue his dreams and give up a future with her? Ruth thought he could have both. Kiev knew differently. He might curb his wanderlust temporarily, but it would return.

Their solution was to release each other to whatever growth was needed. However, the obvious was not always easy to live.

Was it easier for Kiev to release than it was for Ruth?

It seemed that way at the time. He wanted to avoid the heartache his mother had suffered from blaming her husband for all her woes and regrets.

You mean in terms of how Guido forced her to choose between him and you?

I mean in terms of how she told herself that that was what had happened.

Did the time ever come when traveling paled for Kiev?

The time came when a different kind of traveling appealed. Not because the moving got so old, but because the moving got so wonderful, he began to wonder where else it was possible to move to!

Did Kiev run into resistance when he tried to share his ideals?

From the government he did. As the government suppressed new thought, people got curious. Curious people investigated. Therefore, the harder the government tried to purge new thought, the more it spread to the curious.

Did the government manipulate through fear?

Frequently, but the bureaucrats faced their mirrors, too. They used the same tactics that Kiev and his friends were using: *Live as we tell you to or be damned.*

Did you give ultimatums, too?

Not that particular one, but I had issues with the government that brought me close to violence. A friend of mine was crucified. Wanting revenge, I organized a group of protestors to storm the gates of the Senate. I raised my arm to strike a soldier, but caught myself in time, realizing that violence wouldn't solve a thing.

Others used this incident to justify retaliation by saying that I had flown into rages so why shouldn't they? But any time the force of tyranny was at work, those using it were looking for reasons to justify their behavior.

Did you analyze your feelings, Jesus?

Constantly. *Why do I want agreement? Why do I care what others think? Why do I want respect for my ideals?* I finally asked the one question that changed my life forever: *If everyone does agree with me, will I have what I want?* When I knew I wouldn't, I became the person I hoped others would be.

Did Kiev rabble rouse while he was traveling?

Not intentionally, but he came face-to-face with those who believed as strongly as he did that righteousness was on their side. Ironically, action/reaction only computed the idea of righteousness as the gift wanted back by the person who had given it.

Did Kiev idealize you?

As a young man, he did; mostly because he believed that perfection was the ideal. Later, he met a man called Simon who said, *If you truly admire Jesus and want to emulate his path, don't copy the picture he lived, copy the feelings that pulled the two of you together. Then, as you treat others as Jesus treated you, you'll live as one with your idol.*

WHAT YOU CARRY AROUND IN YOUR MIND,
YOU CARRY AROUND IN YOUR MEMORY.
KEEP IT PRODUCTIVE
TO PRODUCE MORE LOVE.

Worksheet Section:

Chapter 20 - Memories

What do you have in your life that brings you constant joy?

Which of those joyful thoughts are not dependent on the moods of those around you?

How does this gift make you feel?

This is your identity. Are you nurturing it?

How can you nurture it more?

Questions to ponder:

- *Am I chasing after someone else's creativity or making the most of my own?*
- *Do I spend all my time justifying my position or do I use my position to love?*
- *Do I question the value of life or do I live a life of value?*

QUESTION NOT
WHAT OTHERS NEED TO KNOW,
ONLY IF YOU KNOW
WHAT BRINGS MORE LOVE TO YOU.

Personal Insights

Kiev and I both had painful memories. I never saw that pain as controllable; I thought it controlled me. Even after I took responsibility for my emotions, memories continued to haunt me. I had to release them over and over. Ego used every trick in the book to keep me static: *Awful memories are with you whether you want them or not; good memories are few and far between; the mind remembers what it wants to remember and you can't change that fact.* On and on it went, telling me whatever it thought would keep me sad and resentful. I finally realized that, if I could keep those painful memories around me year after year, I could jolly well keep the good ones around instead.

CHAPTER 21

Confusion

Why do we get confused?

**KNOWLEDGE OF SELF IS
THE ULTIMATE GOAL.
TO THINK OTHERWISE IS
TO FEEL CONFLICTED.**

What confused you the most, Jesus?

A belief that the quality of my life depended on the actions of others. I wasn't alone in my dilemma; many shared it. Nevertheless, I lived my painful mirrors. Then I picked myself up and tried again until I realized that every emotional action determined my experience.

Who else around you lived in some confusion?

My tailor, Philip, lived in some confusion since he believed that his disrespectful children were the reason he was miserable. When he mentioned his dilemma to me, I said, *To earn their respect, Philip, you have to understand what respect means to you. Then, you have to give your definition so you can receive your definition.*

He listened, but because he thought the problem was his children's to solve, not his to solve, he created more rules for them to follow. He never enforced the rules so his children took advantage of him every chance they got, curious as to why he made the rules in the first place.

Perhaps Phillip wasn't forceful enough when dealing with his children.

Perhaps he wasn't, but to be more forceful, he had to behave as he hoped they would. *Do as I say and ignore what I do* was to teach his children hypocrisy. Even more confusing to Philip was their responsiveness to me. When he asked me why his children listened to my requests and not to his, I told him that he'd have to pay more attention to their requests before they would honor his.

Was Philip an honest tailor?

He wanted to be. When the work piled up, it seemed a lot easier to lose a little honesty than to lose a little business. He demonstrated these values when an unkempt man came into his shop one day. Reluctant to credit a nomad's patronage with the same respect he gave to VIPs, he tossed the order aside as if to say, *I'm too busy to deal with the likes of you.*

Instead of admitting to the customer that he couldn't deliver on the date requested, he let the man believe that his order would be ready. *What do I care if he's inconvenienced?* he thought. *He's a nobody.*

When the customer returned, Philip gave him a long list of excuses to explain his delay. The man didn't believe him, but what could he do at that point except come back when told to.

The children mirrored Philip's behavior that very evening, breaking a promise to do a chore for him, with a long list of excuses to explain their delay. Philip's inability to accept these two situations as balanced justice kept him confused for years. But action/reaction didn't read his relationships in terms of age, gender, or family affiliation; action/reaction read his emotion and reciprocated. Therefore, as Philip inconvenienced and lied to someone, he was inconvenienced and lied to.

Was Philip intentionally rude to this man?

That depends on what you call intentional. Outwardly, he was wooden but polite. Inwardly, he was sizing the customer up in terms of future potential, wondering how much baloney he would endure in the process. How rude do you think that was?

Not rude if the customer was unaware.

But very rude if he was? What if the customer felt his thoughts, spoken or not?

In terms of action/reaction, the customer must have been rude if he felt Philip's rudeness.

If the customer was hurt by Philip's rudeness, that's true. But even if Philip knew that, how could that help him? His life evolved from his behavior, not the customer's, and likewise for the children. They knew their father as a person who said one thing and lived another. And naturally, they were sizing him up in terms of baloney endurance, too.

If Philip had been honest, would he have wondered how much baloney the man would endure?

If he hadn't given any baloney, why would the subject come up?

What about rating the man's potential?

If his only intention was to honor each order as quickly as possible, why would that be relevant? Philip was free to cater to VIP's if he wanted to, and he was free to work in any order he pleased; especially if he made no promises. That said, his integrity would have been better served by doing the work in the order in which it arrived.

Still, two separate issues had to be resolved. In the first issue, Philip said one thing while meaning another, and so had to cope with the falsehoods of others. In the second issue, he rated a man's worthiness according to his income. Then Philip's income was the means by which others rated him. Granted, both had fallout, but the fallout from each was slightly different.

Philip wanted to feel important; and he thought important

clients would make it happen. But regardless of what he hoped for, he faced his mirror. When he heard me say that a person's station in life was emotional not pictorial, he realized how his own philosophy failed him. And he also realized how he'd failed the drifter whose name turned out to be Mark.

When did Philip meet you?

After he moved to Jerusalem. It became obvious to him when he tried to get a license that the government thought tailoring was a very low priority. Because it was a low priority, the process was long and tedious, full of rules and regulations that had to be adhered to.

Frustrated by the bureaucracy and worried about surviving, Philip blurted out that the system wasn't working too well if he was forced to starve rather than offer his services. The clerk snickered. *For equal treatment,* he said, *you'll have to go to Jesus of Nazareth; the government doesn't issue any.*

Out on the street again, Philip asked a passerby if he knew this Jesus of Nazareth. The man introduced himself as Matthew and said, yes, Jesus was a man who traveled the hills of Jerusalem speaking of hearts, heaven, and healing. Liking the sound of that poetry, and with nothing to lose, Philip set out to find me.

When he arrived, I listened to his tale of woe, but instead of offering sympathy, I offered praise: *Even though you suffered at the hands of the clerk, you sensed a deeper meaning behind his words. And because you trusted your feelings over the picture, you found the help you needed.* Then I invited him to present his wares to my friends and acquaintances.

Touched by the offer, Philip asked me why I was so kind to a perfect stranger. I told him we weren't strangers, and when he looked into my eyes he believed it. Thrilled to be back in business, he contributed a percentage of his earnings to the smooth running of my household.

To Philip it was a miracle. He'd arrived in a town that shunned his every effort to succeed, only to meet a man who gave him a new beginning and a chance to expand it. Not by introducing him to a lot of new customers, but by introducing him to the one idea where expansion lived: the willingness to trust oneself.

What had Philip done to attract the mirror of you, Jesus?

He had risked everything in the picture to follow his heart; the nature of the man he met.

Did you appreciate Philip's gift of tailoring?

I did. I wore his garments frequently, admiring his craftsmanship and thanking him daily for his skills.

Did you have time for anything else?

That's what I thought my time was for.

Did Philip appreciate the independence his job gave him?

He appreciated the control it gave him. That's why he had such a hard time with the children. They were rarely controllable.

Was Philip challenged in his adult relationships, too?

Yes, and he sought the cushion of flattery to handle his insecurity. After he married, his wife protected his sensibilities any way she could. In fact, she took her role so seriously, she often incensed the very people Philip was trying to impress. Embarrassed by her zeal, he then had to placate the feelings of those whom she had offended.

Sensing Philip's displeasure, she was confused. Did he want a more vigorous defense, or did he want her withdrawal? After trying the former, she knew he wanted the latter. But instead of liking her non-participation, Philip felt rebuffed by it. Then, convinced that his wife didn't love him the way she used to, he looked for those who would. A no-win situation… but how could it be otherwise if responsibility for self was ignored.

Did Philip want validation?

Yes, he wanted validation, but to ask others to give it was not the way to get it. More importantly, validation wasn't necessary.

When Philip sought my approval, I told him he didn't need it. I also told him that seeking approval would exhaust him as others came seeking his. *Trust your worth,* I told him. *It may not be easy but it's easier than non-trust, a most unpleasant mirror. Think about it, Philip. How can you get to the God within while afraid to trust its presence, afraid to trust its worthiness, and afraid to trust that you are the source of all that is good in your life? Instead of asking for praise, praise your depth.*

Did you have a favorite garment that Philip tailored for you?

Yes, it was a cape that doubled as a blanket. In fact, I had it with me on my way to the crucifixion. When Philip saw the soldier take it away, he wept to distraction. Although he didn't see Vrotskuv return it, he saw it with me later.

Did Philip protect his children from the crucifixion?

No, he couldn't shield them from cruelty; they were often the targets of it. The poor were persecuted and age was no protection. Many children were there to show their love and respect for me.

How did your followers react to your arrest?

Many were angry; either because the officials had taken a stand, or because I had forced the officials to take a stand, or because I was not defending myself, or because they weren't defending me.

What did Philip witness in Jerusalem at the time of the crucifixion?

A city in turmoil; the majority suffering poverty, a small

minority wealth. Soldiers took to the streets daily trying to calm the masses. The government touted reform, but nothing ever developed except for broken promises. Then I came along and promised the people heaven on Earth.

To the government, heaven on Earth meant control of the Earth. Control of the Earth meant power. Power to the people meant less power to the government. To the government, less was unacceptable.

I referred to power as emotional, but those who feared my influence didn't care how I defined it. Their only concern was to get rid of fear.

On the day of the crucifixion, high winds, torrential rains, and ear-splitting noises pummeled the land reflecting the high-strung extremists who blamed the clashing of classes on everything but self-awareness. Philip was frightened until he sensed the meaning behind it all: outer storminess reflecting inner storminess.

Curious as to how I would have responded to this phenomenon, he opened his heart to hear the following message: *The weather is reacting to the force it faces. You can either focus on the positive and reassuring part of this revelation, or you can focus on the panic and terror.*

As the winds blew here and there, every branch, twig, and shrub at the mercy of horrendous gales, he had a choice. He could stay rigid like the twigs that snapped in two, or he could stay flexible like the twigs that bent with the breeze. As the thunder clashed and boomed, he could run for cover, or he could trust the power of action/reaction and sense more power within. As the lightning slashed in blinding fury, he could accept that two immovable objects occupying the same space only united through friction, or he could revel in the brilliance of light interacting with light. As the rain beat down and turned the ground into swampland, he could curse the flooding of homes and businesses, or he could praise the cleansing of all that had masked God's beauty that day.

When the squalls receded, Philip remembered a promise I had made: *My devotion to you is like the sun that always shines, the rain that always purifies, and the river that always flows. In mutual love, we will always be together and nothing in the picture can change it.* Philip lived an epiphany that day and nothing the government did could take it away.

Even though you were removed from the picture, Jesus?

Even though I removed myself from the picture.

How would you define our relationship with nature?

I would call it your most vivid mirror. As the Earth has mutated into this greater mass of atoms, so has the energy living upon its surface. As the Earth has gone from a young and untried organism to a multifaceted kinesis of light and form, so has the energy living that implosion. As nature has lived its many setbacks to reassign priorities, so has the beauty reflecting that path. Through it all, this magnificent core has carried itself with dignity, grace, and a vast amount of love, and so has the holy heart of God embracing that beauty.

YES, YOU ARE ALONE.
BUT IN YOUR ALONENESS YOU ARE ONE.
KEEP THAT ONENESS POSITIVE
AND ALL THAT YOU LONG TO KNOW IS YOURS.

Worksheet Section:

Chapter 21 – Confusion

What in your past has confused you in terms of your journey?

If you named others, begin again.

How has that confusion led to growth?

How has that growth brought you more understanding?

What would you have missed had confusion never come?

Questions to ponder:

- *Do I offer the people around me the best I have to give or the worst I have to give?*
- *Do I trust that people can feel my aura, or do I think that hearts can't feel what eyes can't see?*
- *Do I act accountably every second or do I ask others to account for me?*

BE THE SAME COURTEOUS SOUL TO EVERY LIVING CREATURE TO KNOW THE HEART OF GOD.

Personal Insights

Just as Philip had control issues, I had control issues; mostly because my negative feelings couldn't find expression. The longer I suppressed them, the bigger they seemed to get. The bigger they seemed to get, the more I tried to hide them. When they couldn't release comfortably, they released uncomfortably, and usually when I least expected to feel them!

These days, I deal with negative feelings by taking my cue from nature. Everyday, it expresses through fires, storms, and eruptions, and everyday it begins again to expand the life it is. If I erupt in private, nothing unpleasant develops. I get those feelings out and reclaim my comfort.

CHAPTER 22

Death

Is death real?

GOD IS.
THEREFORE,
GOD IS EVERYTHING.

Were you afraid of death, Jesus?

Death had to be real to be feared. When I knew death was impossible, I couldn't fear something I knew did not exist.

Did you ever fear a person?

Yes, but after I knew that fear was felt from bringing fear to others, I was free to act on my own behalf to source something else.

Who stirred up a lot of fear in the people around you?

Pilate created the kind of panic that most people feared.

The Pilate who had you crucified?

The Pilate who ruled Judea when I conquered hate through the power of love.

Did Pilate conquer hate, too?

No, hate conquered Pilate as Pilate used his hate to conquer others. To justify his hate, he told himself that his enemies were all such horrible monsters, they deserved to die.

Did Pilate have a God he liked to worship?

Yes, but the God he liked to worship was the picture he saw

with his eyes. As the picture became his priority, he wanted the picture to grow. When it didn't grow as fast as he thought it should, he used the punishing side of his nature to make it happen; the God who didn't care, the God who thought he was awful, the God who reasoned as he did.

Wasn't God all-powerful, beautiful, and benevolent?

God was whatever God was. Millions of souls existed and all of them were God. Some were stuck in punitive thought. But no deity was sitting up in heaven, singling out this person and that person to castigate; nor did any deity need to do this. Energy did it for itself by bringing likeness back.

Did hate make Pilate horrible?

Hate made Pilate a person discovering the power of action-emotion.

Wasn't there a God who punished him for his sins?

If such a God existed, how do you think that punishment would have arrived?

Through agony, to punish him for the agony he brought others.

If he suffered for that reason, wouldn't it motivate him to find a different atonement in the future? He lived the pain he inflicted for a good reason: so the force of his reflection would prevent that pain again. Pilate condemned himself to whatever he condemned others to. If hell is what that was, hell is what he experienced.

Someone could have respected him and made him a better person.

Why would that someone have respected Pilate?

Because that person was respectful not rude.

How would Pilate know that?

By how he felt.

He felt what he had given. Pilate sought the respect of others, but he tried to get it by killing those who denied him theirs. Fearful actions created fear the same as respectful actions created respect. And since he could only be in one emotion at the same time unless they were compatible, he decided how to feel by the feelings he gave to others.

Did he think of himself as a big shot?

Yes, and if he lost that sense of importance, he'd lord it over someone until he got it back.

Before Pilate came into his body, what did he feel, what did he want, and who was he?

He was energy; everything he felt was everything he'd been able to give. When he wanted more of a certain emotion, he decided where to find it and acted on his own behalf to get it.

This lifetime was the personification of his desire to know what it meant to emote powerfully, merit recognition, and command respect.

Was he divine energy, even as Pilate?

Yes, and if you understand this one concept, your journey will have been an incredible gift in awareness.

When Pilate killed people, what happened to him emotionally?

The first time he experienced the act of killing, he thought he'd killed himself. The second time, he thought he'd died again. And each time after that, he felt a little deader. When he realized that killing was required in order to keep his job, and he knew that he wouldn't relinquish it without a fight to the death, he resigned himself to a life of cruel behavior.

But along with resignation came a morbid curiosity about those he had condemned. To satisfy his oligarchic interest, he asked his prisoners how they viewed their own impending death. His prisoners, knowing they were doomed anyway, told him what he wanted to know. It turned out that whatever Pilate feared they feared. Whatever he hated they hated. Whatever he loved they loved. Granted, Pilate's picture was not the picture they had, but emotionally, he and his prisoners lived in oneness; all of them believing that after the picture was gone, life was over.

Did Pilate feel compassion for these souls?

There were times when he did, but Pilate told himself that in order to keep his job, he had to be stronger, wilier, and more powerful than anyone else around him. Fear and intimidation were the tools that made him successful. As punishing mirrors returned, compassion was hard to find. And without any proof of compassion in him, he couldn't trust it elsewhere.

Maybe he would have tried harder to be a better person had he known his real identity.

Maybe he lived whatever would help him to recognize the God he was.

Did Pilate react to the rumor that you were God?

Not at first. As far as he was concerned, I was just another Haggai; the country was full of them, and they all had something inflammatory to say. He reasoned that if God existed, he would be the ultimate. The ultimate would know how to wield great power. In Pilate's world, power referred to the picture. In the picture, I had none.

Later, when the masses got behind me, Pilate reassessed. But even then, he had no personal grudge against me. On the contrary, he was somewhat sympathetic. Here was a perfectly nice man with no understanding of the ways the world. But amazingly, he was willing to teach me. *Nothing to it*, he thought.

Give Jesus what he needs to appease his thirst for power and all my problems are solved.

When I told Pilate that the ways of the world didn't interest me, he was surprised. *How am I supposed to help you if you won't listen to reason?* I responded that I had no expectation of help.

An odd answer, Pilate thought. He was used to people trying to talk themselves out of trouble, and he was used to the feeling of power it gave him.

Did Pilate accuse you of leading the people to rebel against the government?

Yes, and he thought I was. Many rebels were claiming me as their leader. When he mentioned this, I didn't deny their rebellion, but I said they were leading themselves. I wouldn't take responsibility for their behavior any more than I expected Pilate to take responsibility for mine.

Did you say that you were God?

I said that everyone was God, and that Pilate might learn something interesting from taking responsibility for the God he was being. Pilate didn't think God visited him, and if God visited me, I had to die. The seat of power was not up for grabs.

When I told him that death had no reality, he wanted to prove me wrong. After the crucifixion, he thought he had. After the resurrection he panicked. *What have I done? What does it mean? What did I do?* Ego had a field day. *See,* it said, *he was God. Hate yourself. Feel miserable. Feel unclean.*

Confused and frightened, he rationalized the role he'd played in this drama. But to participate in a person's death was to kill a body that one God thought informative. And since everyone is one, he killed a part of himself in the process.

Did he hate himself for supporting the crucifixion?

Yes, but hate kept him out of reality. And since answers

resided in reality, looking for answers outside of it was the ultimate frustration.

Couldn't he have gone to someone for help?

Pilate wasn't open to receiving help. People didn't trust him, and with good reason.

What did this lifetime teach him?

That he was God in the everything he chose.

If he'd known that as Pilate, would it have made any difference?

I'm sure he would have been thrilled to know that every effort was meaningful.

When he returned in another lifetime, did he succumb to the same old vanities?

Oh he had plenty of vanities to deal with but the growth he'd found as Pilate helped him to sense what he didn't want to get stuck in again.

How could he remember that from one lifetime to another?

How could he not remember that if his reality was emotional?

How could he keep his memory of that reality once he was back in form?

By taking the same idea and putting it in a familiar one. Would he purposefully perpetrate a painful experience one day that he had lived the day before?

No, but one was about gaping lifetimes, the other about yesterday and today.

What was the difference between Pilate's emotion at ten and his emotion at thirty?

What he felt in between.

Same with lifetimes.

How could eons be compared to a day?

In terms of "time" it couldn't be. But the soul didn't live in time; it lived in emotion. To Pilate's soul, one moment was more meaningful than eons if something wonderful was happening in it.

Did he have any good intentions?

He had many good intentions, but good intentions only got him the good intentions of others. He had to "do" in order to have. For instance, what would have happened had he only intended to kill?

Okay, I see what you mean, but what if he wanted proof that action/reaction worked?

Then he had to look to his life for the proof he needed: fear came from giving fear, stress came from giving stress, judgment came from giving judgment. That was the only proof he'd ever find.

Were you stressed, Jesus, when you had your meeting with Pilate?

No, but only because my definition of stress was not the same as his. To me, it meant to be halfway in my beliefs and therefore ineffectual using them. To be stress-free, I had to honor my theories wherever I was, not just in certain situations with certain people.

I saw my life as an emotional experience. Therefore, I gave the love, consideration, and kindness I deserved instead of the lack of faith Pilate deserved. Then, any threats from him were meaningless; I controlled my fate when it came to feelings.

Can you elaborate on what it meant to be halfway in your beliefs?

It meant to be living them only when the picture was supportive. To live them fully was to live them even when the picture was not supportive.

Did Pilate find answers when he dropped his body?

He found opportunities through which to seek them. No other God could tell him where to find them since no other God had that information, and for good reason; only Pilate knew what he needed to feel. But regardless of any help he received along the way, using it effectively was still up to him.

He must have felt so alone.

He was alone in terms of finding new ideas, but once he knew how capable he was of moving from one to another, he joined all those in parallel thinking.

Did Pilate make any wrong decisions?

He made loveless decisions. But all choices were worthy in the context of growth; therefore all choices were valid. After he left this journey, his soul planned another; then another, and yet another one after that. In each of these incarnations he lived what he had judged before. Eventually he chose a lifetime in which all of his previous choices paid off.

But his payoff was emotional, not pictorial. Pilate had to look for the best in others, not the worst. The way he viewed humanity was the way he viewed himself; and the way he viewed himself determined his future.

WORDS GO NOWHERE.
FEELINGS EMPOWER.
ACTION CREATES.

Worksheet Section:

Chapter 22 - Death

Why do you experience stress?

If you blamed others, try again.

Where have you given stress?

What would you rather have instead?

Give your preference and watch it all come back.

Questions to Ponder:

- *Am I worried about death or am I making the most of life?*
- *Am I someone I'd like to meet, or someone I'd like to avoid?*
- *Am I honoring now as the moment of import or wishing the future would hurry up and arrive?*

THE WORST THAT HAS EVER BEEN IS STILL A MOMENT OF BRILLIANCE.

Personal Insights

For years, I thought of God as separate; a force that lived outside of me instead of within my heart. Then I created problems. First of all, I depended on God to get me out of pickles when I was the one who created them. I expected God to forgive me for all my sins while I was the one who needed to forgive myself. I prayed for God to change the way I was living while I was the one who decided how it would be. I prayed for God to rid me of all diseases while I was the one who held dis-eased thoughts. I prayed for God to bless my family and friends while I was the one who either blessed their presence or didn't. I prayed for God to create a peaceful world while I was the one who needed peace within. I prayed for God to win me a victory over my enemies while I was the one I warred against.

CHAPTER 23

Time

Why are we living in time?

"BEING"
IS AUTOMATIC.
IN THE PROCESS OF BEING,
ENERGY EXPERIMENTS.

Did you think of yourself as energy experimenting, Jesus?

By the time I met Herod, I did. And I knew he was experimenting, too, in terms of how he felt about me: should he trust his heart or should he trust his friends. At first, he trusted his heart. When he lost his friends from trusting his heart, he did the expedient.

Was that a tragedy?

No, it was research. He was here to learn like everyone else.

What if he wasted his time while experimenting?

What if he entered time in order to experiment and, therefore, wasted his time when he didn't?

What if he cost the lives of others because he was experimenting?

What if others were experimenting, too?

How would you describe Herod's life?

As mental, physical, and architectural: mental in that human nature intrigued him; physical in that bodily health obsessed him; and architectural in that civic improvements challenged him.

Psychological research evolved as he did; fitness programs improved as his did; and civic improvements depended on several weighty factors: the accessibility of artisans; the capriciousness of nature; and the availability of funds.

If the costs became prohibitive, and negative deficits outnumbered public benefits, he heeded his staff and put the projects on hold. But once a decision was made, he found it difficult to reverse it, even when his instincts told him he should.

Did he want to live responsibly as a person who followed-through?

Yes, but to live responsibly was to follow his instincts.

Maybe his instincts weren't all that accurate.

What better reason to come here and test them?

Did he enjoy the picture of being Herod?

He enjoyed the power it gave him, and since no other picture offered that power, he strove to keep it around.

Did he kill innocents like Pilate killed innocents?

If you mean, did he allow children to be killed, yes, but all godly souls were living a path of insight, even innocents.

Did Pilate live his karma by returning in another lifetime as an innocent who was murdered?

He became the parent of an innocent who was murdered. But his soul didn't make choices to bring itself more suffering; it made choices to end suffering.

In the context of that sentence, growth seems to be cruel.

Was it cruel to learn to swim so drowning didn't happen? Learning might have been difficult but it was certainly worth the effort. In the big picture of growth, Herod came here to experience the thrill of accomplishment. Therefore, he took a path that offered that opportunity. He also hoped to remember that his life was not worth living if the joy of life was gone.

Did Herod consider himself a highly skilled leader?

He considered himself a highly skilled manipulator and, to tell you the truth, he was happy to have that skill; it usually got him exactly what he wanted. After he manipulated, he got uneasy. After all, if he'd gotten what he wanted by manipulating others, why wouldn't others try to manipulate him to get what they wanted.

Were his projects philanthropic?

Most of them were, and he hoped that thousands of people would enjoy them, not only for their outer beauty, but also for their mental, physical, and emotional opportunities.

Did Herod seek you out, Jesus?

Yes; our meeting was inevitable. I was offering a self-improvement program of my own. As thousands became aware of it, the men around Herod, who made a living by pleasing him, began to worry. *What if those thousands become tens of thousands? And what if Jesus' influence undermines ours?* Afraid that that might happen, they did their best to discredit me, resurrecting my history to make me appear a threat.

Herod heard them out. But accustomed to those who felt under siege, he reassured his colleagues that although I had once been political, times had changed and so had I. Not so easily appeased, these men sought guarantees. In an effort to give them, Herod assigned a deputy to further investigate any and all activities to which I had lent my name.

The deputy reported back that I was not competitive, nor were the words I spoke inflammatory. Confident he'd done his duty, he reiterated to his colleagues that I was preaching peace. Instead of feeling pacified, these men felt ignored. In their opinion, Herod had only concluded that my ministry was not a threat to him. What about their solidarity? What if Herod turned against them in favor of me; especially if I controlled the masses?

Annoyed by their skepticism, Herod looked into the matter himself and, in disguise, came to hear me speak. What he discovered confirmed his belief that I was not a threat. Then he was confused. Why were his colleagues so worried about me, and what did they see in me that he did not?

In an effort to calm their fears, Herod repeated what he had said before, that I was a peaceful man, preaching peace to others. Not satisfied to let the matter rest, his colleagues schemed behind Herod's back, stirring up trouble with other political factions; factions Herod could not ignore.

If not for the grumblings in the Senate and the growing discontent of the masses, Herod would have ignored these doubting colleagues and dropped them from his agenda. But the controversy grew to such an extent that he either had to respond with leadership or forfeit some of his own.

Did you say anything in your sermon that made Herod feel good about himself?

I said a great deal that made him feel good about himself.

Then why did he care if the masses listened?

He didn't; he thought I was harmless. His aides, however, considered me a menace; someone encouraging the masses to feel powerful, capable, and independent. They didn't want the masses feeling powerful. They wanted them feeling subservient; sure of being at the mercy of a benevolent bureaucracy.

Outnumbered, Herod had to take a stand. He started from strength and did what any master manipulator would do: offer me a job. *All you have to do*, he said, *is convince the masses that the government wants to help the rich and poor alike*. I thanked him for his faith in me and declined.

Surprised, Herod asked for an explanation. I replied that the government didn't care about the masses. *Good heavens,* he thought, *if this is his reason for declining, he must want a better offer.* So he upped the ante and increased the pay. I told him that money was not the reward I sought.

Irritated, but by no means discouraged, Herod dug deeper. Concede here, take there, wrap things up; that's usually how it worked. He held all the aces, didn't he?

So when I showed no interest in money, he offered me power and prestige. No words were needed this time. Herod read the message in my eyes. *If power and prestige are so desirable, then why do I feel such sadness in you?*

Disliking the direction of the conversation, and annoyed at my rejection of an easy escape, Herod came up with another offer: Life. *How stubborn will you be looking death in the eye?* he asked. I told him I didn't believe in death anymore; therefore, I'd be steadfast. That took Herod aback. He wasn't used to blasé attitudes regarding death. In the past, that was always the ace that won the game.

When I didn't so much as a flinch, he got disgusted. Here he was wasting all this time on a lowly Haggai; a minor issue on his agenda. Anxious to end the meeting, he warned me that if I didn't come up with better answers soon, I wouldn't live out the fortnight.

As the guard approached me, Herod rose and walked toward his living quarters, glancing over his shoulder to wave me out. His arm froze in mid-air as he looked into my eyes. Instead of seeing the fear he expected, he saw only love.

Impossible, Herod thought, *not in this situation.* Stunned, he lost his focus. In fact, he couldn't believe the message he was receiving. *You are the love of God regardless of what you decide for.* Flummoxed, he stood there, unable to break eye contact until a servant broke the spell.

As Herod reflected on our meeting, he got uneasy. *What just occurred between the two of us? The message didn't compute. Nothing I said to Jesus warranted love; just the opposite. But he was totally serene and peaceful, and completely adoring of me.*

Later, he told a friend about this meeting. She teased him saying that I had gotten the better of him. Was she right? Would others hear of this meeting and believe that a lowly Haggai had out-maneuvered Herod? Unwilling to take that chance, he conceded to the wishes of his colleagues, and arranged for a trial where I would be judged on the grounds of seditious behavior. At the very least, he hoped his pride would be restored.

The trial began and Herod asked me to state my beliefs; particularly those regarding death. He hoped that given the opportunity, I would crucify myself. I repeated what I'd been saying all along; that death had to be real to be feared. My reality was life.

The court was mildly surprised and somewhat amused; certainly not intimidated. *What's the big deal here?* A few even tittered, likening me to a child in mistaken beliefs.

Herod understood; his reaction had been the same. But these men, now feigning ignorance, were the ones who had pushed him to take a stand. Suspicious of their motives and feeling under siege, he overreacted and demanded a crucifixion. The court resisted; sure that the man in front of them was not the dangerous criminal they'd been led to believe.

Sensing their reluctance, Herod used the same strategy his colleagues had used on him, and spoke of the rebellion that, at one time, had defined my growth. *Is this what you want*, he asked the courtroom, *someone leading the masses to revolution*? Revolution was not a word these men wanted to hear. But suggesting that the man in front of them could create it seemed absurd. Feeling that his support was fast eroding, Herod taunted me, hoping to elicit out-of-control behavior. I responded calmly, answering every question put to me until Herod appeared the fanatic. Frustrated, he asked me if I was just too stupid to sense my fate. I said that perhaps he should stop worrying so much about my fate and have more concern for his.

Worried that I might be mocking him, and furious at his colleagues for jumping ship, Herod took a stand he would later regret. At the time, it seemed like the only way he could save face. The people he trusted the most were playing him for a fool. He either had to push for a verdict he didn't want, or lose his credibility.

Adding insult to injury, he felt the contentment in me that he had always been seeking. When he saw no reason for me to have it, he felt enraged. Then, he demanded a harsh judgment to demonstrate that he was the one in charge here, not his wavering cohorts.

After the crucifixion, Herod felt better. I'd said that death was impossible but I had died. When I came back three days later, Herod didn't feel so good any more.

Are you saying that Herod saw you?

I'm saying that hundreds of people saw me. Those like Herod didn't want the facts repeated. Therefore, they made a concerted effort to kill the truth. As they did, the facts got distorted.

Why did you show yourself to hundreds instead of just the faithful?

Why would the faithful need to see me? I wanted to be seen by the likes of Herod, those who had no faith, those who had no serenity, and those who had no security.

Did Herod speak to you upon your return?

No, but he heard me speak. During those moments he was open to the love he felt. In the days that followed, ego tormented him with fear, anxiety, and self-loathing. Self-loathing did him in. But he took what he had learned this lifetime into the next one. And, having lived those moments of peace in my presence, he was able to expand them.

Eventually, Herod realized that death did not exist; it was only a thought believed in and therefore reflected in the picture.

Did he realize this while he was still Herod?

No, he realized this when his energy moved on.

What happened in Herod's heart in the meeting he had with you?

Inexplicably, Rome, politics, and position suddenly became irrelevant; he was able to sense a depth in himself he hadn't known existed. Yes, he suppressed freedom, killed his enemies, patronized the poor, and martyred innocents, but he also felt the beauty in others and responded. He couldn't maintain that awareness in the days that followed. In fact, he betrayed it again and again. Nevertheless, it was his for a few time-stopping moments. Therefore, it was his into eternity.

TO BE SOMEBODY,
IS TO TRUST THE SOMEBODY
YOU ARE.

Worksheet Section:

Chapter 23 - Time

What do you value in life?

Which of those assets transcend illusion?

How are you allowing this beauty to flourish?

How can you share it with others?

Who will you be as you do?

Questions to ponder:

- *Do I enter into relationships to cherish the people I find or to dominate the people I find?*
- *Do I try to awaken inner power or try to find outer power?*
- *Do I focus on all that is right in others or focus on all that is wrong?*

EVEN IN MOMENTS OF SUPRESSED SENSITIVITY, ENERGY IS BEAUTIFUL.

Personal Insights

I love that we come here to experiment in time. When you think about it, time is a curious subject. As we age, it feels like time speeds up, even though logic tells us that children experience the same time, and for them it goes very slowly.

Does time speed up because it's illusionary and, therefore, a tool to be used in whatever way the user needs to use it? Children need for time to go slowly. There is much to learn in their new environment. Adults, on the other hand, familiar with their surroundings, are more philosophical. *Why am I here? What is my purpose? How can I grow?*

Perhaps time speeds up as the focus narrows down. Often the elderly use their time to reflect: another kind of measurement. But each phase is perfect for the person who is living it. Maybe the most we can hope for is that we use our time in a way that makes the next phase worthy.

LOVE IS NEVER APPRECIATED UNTIL YOU'VE WORKED HARD TO KEEP IT AROUND.

The Research

Walking Through Illusion is not a supplement to another book; it's a supplement to the heart. It offers an emotional accounting of what might have been, not a historical accounting. But in an effort to bring the two together, the following research was done.

In the Bible(1), Peter, Andrew, John, Philip, Bartholomew, Thomas, Matthew, Thaddeus, and Judas are mentioned as apostles(2).

In **Walking Through Illusion**, the lives of these men are discussed in terms of what they might have felt as they lived their journeys and understood their challenges. However, similarities to The Bible exist.

Bartholomew is a martyr in **Walking Through Illusion,** as he is in the Bible. In one version of The Bible, he was beheaded; in another, he was flayed and crucified(3).

The Bible portrays Peter as a fisherman, along with his brother, Andrew(4), and it also speaks of the fact that Peter denied his friendship with Jesus(5). Jona is the name of Peter and Andrew's father in The Bible as well(6).

In **Walking Through Illusion**, Paul is a tax collector; a man of business engaged in several occupations–one of them being tent maker. The Bible mentions his association with the latter(7). As a young man, Paul's personality in **Walking Through Illusion** tends toward self-righteousness. The behavior of Paul in The Bible supports this supposition(8). The Bible also mentions that Paul had a vision of sorts(9) and speaks of his participation in several missionary journeys(10).

Matthew, son if Alphaeus(11), also known as Levi in the Book of Luke(12), is documented in The Bible. Further information about him is sparse, but he is mentioned as sitting at "the receipt of custom" indicating a government job(13).

Mark is known as a traveling man in **Walking Through Illusion**. Although The Bible offers little information about his life, his presence is noted at several locations(14), and some consider him an eyewitness to Peter's preaching(15).

John the Baptist is in The Bible(16), but his early years are undocumented(17). Biblical verses mention his relationship with Herod, as well as his death(18).

The Bible confirms that Thomas was a doubter(19) and also that he was known as a friend of Jesus'(20). This book takes the concept of doubt to a deep and spiritual level as Thomas learns to accept himself for the gift he has to offer.

The resurrection of Lazarus, as well as his friendship with Jesus is documented in The Bible(21). It also refers to Lazarus as the brother of Mary Magdalene(22).

Judas is mentioned in The Bible as the man who betrayed Jesus(23). His suicide is also cited, although The Bible has two versions that account for how it happened(24).

Besides the previously named Apostles, Mary Magdalene is seen in the presence of Jesus and his family(25). In the Book of Luke, she is said to have been healed of evil spirits(26).

The Bible speaks of Pilate and Herod as they dealt with Jesus, as well as their relationship with each other(27).

In terms of other characters in this book such as Kaleb and Vrotskuv, there is no biblical reference to them, but references are made to different miracles(28), and to the fact that Jesus encountered soldiers on his way to the crucifixion(29).

Finally, I would ask you to consider that the true research for this book was done in my heart. I hope that my discoveries have, in some way, touched yours in a meaningful way.

End Notes

1. The Holy Bible, King James Version (Nashville: Broadman & Holman Publishers, 1979)

2. Now the names of the twelve Apostles are these; the first Simon, who is called Peter, and Andrew his brother, James *the son* of Zebedee, and John his brother; (Matthew 10:2)

Philip, and Bartholomew; Thomas, and Matthew the publican; James *the son* of Alphaeus, and Lebbaeus, whose surname was Thaddaeus; (Matthew 10:3)

Simon the Canaanite, and Judas Iscariot, who also betrayed him. (Matthew 10:4)

3. He is said to have died in Albanopolis, Armenia, but stories of his death differ; according to one, he was beheaded; others state that he was flayed alive and crucified. (http://www.newadvent.org.cathen/02313c.htm)

4. And Jesus, walking by the sea of Galilee, saw two brethren, Simon called Peter, and Andrew his brother, casting a net into the sea: for they were fishers. (Matthew 4:18)

Now as he walked by the sea of Galilee, he saw Simon and Andrew his brother casting a net into the sea: for they were fishers. (Mark 1:16)

5. And the second time the cock drew. And Peter called to mind the word that Jesus said unto him, Before the cock crow twice, thou shalt deny me thrice. And when he thought thereon, he wept. (Mark 14:72)

6. And he brought him to Jesus. And when Jesus beheld him, he said, Thou art Simon the son of Jona: thou shalt be called Cephas, which is by interpretation A Stone. (John 1:42)

7. And because he [Paul] was of the same craft, he abode with them, and wrought: for by their occupation they were tentmakers. (Acts 18:3)

8. And Saul [Saul is Paul in Hebrew, Page 8 in the Bible Dictionary in the back of the Kind James Version], yet breathing out threatenings and slaughter against the disciples of the Lord, went unto the high priest, (Acts 9:1)

9. And he fell to the earth, and heard a voice saying unto him, Saul, Saul [Saul is Paul in Hebrew], why persecutest though me? (Acts 9: 4)

And he said, Who art thou Lord? And the Lord said, I am Jesus whom thou persecutest: *it is* hard for thee to kick against the pricks. (Acts 9: 5)

10. Now when Paul and his company loosed from Paphos, they came to Perga in Pamphylia: and John departing from them returned to Jerusalem. (Acts 13: 13)

But when they departed from Perga, they came to Antioch in Pisidia, and when into the synagogue on the Sabbath day, and sat down. (Acts 13: 14)

And after he [Paul] had spend some time *there*, he departed, and went over *all* the country of Galatia and Phrygia in order, strengthening all the disciples. (Acts 18:23)

11. And as he [Jesus] passed by, he saw Levi [Matthew], the *son*

of Alphaeus sitting at the receipt of custom, and said unto him, Follow me. And he arose and followed him. (Mark 2:14)

12. The Holy Bible, King James Version (Nashville: Broadman & Holman Publishers, 1979) Page 6 of the Bible Dictionary section in the back of the book.

13. And as Jesus passed forth from thence, he saw a man, named Matthew, sitting at the receipt of custom: and he saith unto him, Follow me. And he arose, and followed him. (Matthew 9:9)

Matthew, "Son of Alphaeus, he lived at Capenaum on Lake Genesareth. He was a Roman tax collector, a position equated with collaboration with the enemy by those from whom he collected taxes."
(http://www.catholic-forum.com/saints/saintm13.htm)

14. And Barnabas determined to take with them John, whose surname was Mark. (Acts 15:37)

And the contention was so sharp between them, that they departed asunder one from the other: and so Barnabas took Mark, and sailed into Cyprus. (Acts 15:39)

Now when Paul and his company loosed from Paphos, they came to Perga in Pamphylia: and John [Mark] departing from them returned to Jerusalem. (Acts 13:13)

15. "Mark is considered an eyewitness or the recorder of Peter's preaching."
(http://www.geocities.com/Athens/Forum/2736/faq.html)

16. That word, *I say*, ye know, which was published throughout all Judaea, and began from Galilee, after the baptism which John

preached; (Acts 10:37)

Then remembered I the word of the Lord, how that he said. John indeed baptized with water; but ye shall be baptized with the Holy Ghost. (Acts 11:16)

When John had first preached before his coming the baptism of repentance to all the people of Israel. (Acts 13:24)

17. "and [John] lived in seclusion until AD 26."
(http://www.sacklunch.net/biography/J/JohntheBaptist_1.html)

"He withdrew into the harsh, rocky desert beyond the Jordan to fast and pray,"
(http://www.directessays.com/viewpaper/48899.html)

18. For Herod had laid hold of John [the Baptist], and bound him, and put *him* in prison for Herodias' sake, his brother Philip's wife. (Matthew 14:3)

For John said unto him, It is not lawful for thee to have her. (Matthew 14:4)

And when he would have put him to death, he feared the multitude, because they counted him a prophet. (Matthew 14:5)

But when Herod's birthday was kept, the daughter of Herodias danced before them, and pleased Herod. (Matthew 14:6)

Whereupon he promised with an oath to give her whatsoever she would ask. (Matthew 14:7)

And she, being before instructed of her mother, said, Give me here John Baptist's head in a charger. (Matthew 14:8)

And the king was sorry: nevertheless for the oath's sake, and them which sat with him at meat, he commanded *it* to be given *her*. (Matthew 14:9)

And he sent, and beheaded John in the prison. (Matthew 14:10)

19. Thomas saith unto him, Lord, we know not whither thou goest; and how can we know the way? (John 14:5)

But Thomas, one of the twelve, called Didymus, was not with them when Jesus came. (John 20:24)

The other disciples therefore said unto him, We have seen the Lord. But he said unto them, Except I shall see in his hands the print of the nails, and put my finer on the print of his nails, and thrust my hand into his side, I will not believe. (John 20:25)

And after eight days again his disciples were within, and Thomas with them: *then* came Jesus, the doors being shut, and stood in the midst, and said, Peace *be* unto you. (John 20:26)

Then saith he to Thomas, Reach hither thy finger, and behold my hands; and reach hither thy hand, and thrust *it* into my side: and be not faithless, but believing. (John 20:27)

And Thomas answered and said unto him, My Lord and my God. (John 20:28)

Jesus saith unto him, Thomas, because thou hast seen me, thou hast believed: blessed *are* they that have not seen, and *yet* have believed. (John 20: 29)

20. Then said Thomas, which is called Didymus, unto his fellowdisciples, Let us also go, that we may die with him. (John

11:16)

21. Then Jesus six days before the passover came to Bethany, where Lazarus was which had been dead, whom he raised from the dead. (John 12:1)

22. (It was that Mary [Magdalene] which anointed the Lord with ointment, and wiped his feet with her hair, whose brother Lazarus was sick.) (John 11: 2)

23. Then saith one of his disciples, Judas Iscariot, Simon's son, which should betray him, (John 12:4

Simon the Canaanite, and Judas Iscariot, who betrayed him. (Matthew 10:4)

And Judas Iscariot, which also betrayed him: and they went into an house. (Mark 3:19)

24. And he cast down the pieces of silver in the temple, and departed, and went and hanged himself. (Matthew 27.5)

Now this man [Judas] purchased a field with the reward of iniquity; and falling head long, he burst asunder in the midst, and all his bowels gushed out. (Acts 1:18)

25. The first *day* of the week cometh Mary Magdalene early, when it was yet dark, unto the sepulchre, and seeth the stone taken away from the sepulchre. (John 20:1)

There were also women looking on afar off: among whom was Mary Magdalene, and Mary the mother of James the less and Joses, and Salome; (Mark 15:40)

In the end of the sabbeth, as it began to dawn toward the first *day* of the week, came Mary Magdalene and the other Mary to see the sepulchre. (Matthew 28:1)

26. And certain women, which has been healed of evil spirits and infirmities, Mary called Magdalene, out of whom went seven devils, (Luke 8:2)

27. And when they had bound him [Jesus], they led him away, and delivered him to Pontius Pilate the governor. (Matthew 27:2)

And the whole multitude of them arose, and led him to Pilate. (Luke 23:1)

And they began to accuse him, saying, We found this *fellow* perverting the nation, and forbidding to give tribute to Caesar, saying that he himself is Christ a King. (Luke 23:2)

And Pilate asked him, saying, Art thou the King of the Jews? And he answered him and said, Thou sayest it. (Luke 23:3)

Then said Pilate to the chief priests and to the people, I find no fault in this man. (Luke 23:4)

And they were more fierce, saying, He stirreth up the people, teaching throughout all Jewry, beginning from Galilee to this place. (Luke 23:5)

When Pilate heard of Galilee, he asked whether the man was a Galilaean. (Luke 23:6)

And as soon as he knew that he belonged unto Herod's jurisdiction, he sent him to Herod, who himself also was at Jerusalem at that time. (Luke 23: 7)

And Herod with his men of war set him at nought, and mocked *him*, and arrayed him in a gorgeous robe, and sent him again to Pilate. (Luke 23: 11)

Pilate saith unto him, what is truth? And when he said this, he went out again unto the Jews, and saith unto them, I find in him no fault at all. (John 18:38)

28. The beginning of miracles did Jesus in Cana of Galilee, and manifested forth his glory; and his disciples believed on him. (John 2:11)

And they were all amazed, insomuch that they questioned among themselves, saying, What thing is thing is this? what new doctrine *is* this? for with authority commandeth he [Jesus] even the unclean spirits, and they do obey him. (Mark 1:27)

And immediately he [the man with palsy] arose, took up the bed, and went forth before them all; insomuch that they were all amazed, and glorified God, saying, We never saw it on this fashion. (Mark 2: 12)

And looking around about them all, he [Jesus] said unto the man [with a withered hand], Stretch for they hand. And he did so: and his hand was restored whole as the other. (Luke 6: 10)

29. And the soldiers platted a crown of thorns, and put *it* on his [Jesus] head, and they put on him a purple robe, (John 19: 2)